Ten Months in Iran
or
God wants me to kill you.

By: J. F. Simpson

To Helena Karvonen

John F Simpson

A Rubric Publications Book

Ten Months in Iran

Copyright © 2004 by John F. Simpson

All rights reserved. No part of this book may be reproduced, copied or transmitted in any form or by any means without written permission from the publisher except for approved advertising and where permitted by law.

ISBN 0-9755099-0-X

Printed in India

First Edition May 2004

http://www.rubricpublications.com

Ten Months in Iran

This book is dedicated to the loyal officers and men of the Imperial Iranian Army and Air Force who were murdered under orders from the Ayatollah.

Ten Months in Iran

Published by
Rubric Publishing Inc.
7040 W Plametto Pk Rd, Ste 4, PMB 542
Boca Raton, Florida 33433-3483

Ten Months in Iran

Preface

In the spring if 1978 I went to work for Bell Helicopter as a test pilot in Isfahan, Iran. My assignment was to test fly helicopters and serve as an instructor for Iranian army personal assigned to flight operations. I was in Iran until late December of 1978. This is my account of the events that took place prior to the collapse of the Shah's government, the short period of anarchy that followed the Shah's departure and the return of Ayatollah Khomeini. It also presents my thoughts about radical Shiite Muslim practices and customs that I observed. The names I use in this book are not the actual names of the people involved; I changed the names to protect the people I knew and the woman I loved from the psychological torment and physical punishment the clerical dictatorship of Iran would surely inflect upon them.

I wish I could say that everyone I knew and cared for in Iran survived and escaped to safety; but, I know from news and TV reports that some of the Iranian army officers I became acquainted with and liked, many of whom were educated in the United States, were executed by orders from the cleric dictator Ayatollah Khomeini. In the years since the Ayatollah's takeover of the Iranian

Ten Months in Iran

government, thousands of intellectual and military leaders have been executed as part of the Ayatollah's cleansing process of the Iranian Muslim culture. I also found out, through Iranian friends who visited Iran after the Iran-Iraq war, that the children of some of my friends were drafted and subsequently killed in the Iran-Iraq war; when I knew them they were bright young teen and pre-teen boys looking forward to college in the United States, England or France.

As I write this book we are at war with Iraq to remove a despot from power; if we aren't very careful one of Iraq's rogue Muslim clerics will incite his followers to attack the infidel invaders and plunge Iraq into a civil war. A civil war in Iraq could result in the establishment of a cleric dictatorship similar to the one the Ayatollah set up in Iran. If we give up Iraq again to another despot, we will be back in another ten years doing it all over again and our soldiers and those of the United Kingdom will have died in vain. The enemy in Iraq, after the shooting stops, will be the rogue Muslim clerics who will incite the population against our troops.

The Islamic clerics of Iran and Afghanistan have corrupted, distorted and misrepresented the teachings of the Qur'an to such an extent that any true Muslim must be appalled by their conduct. In the words of a Muslim friend of mine, "they've hijacked Islam and appended their ancient tribal customs to the Qur'an in an attempt to validate their beliefs; and, they have done all of this for their own personal gain and to maintain control of the Muslim populations of backward countries".

Ten Months in Iran

**Prolog
December 1978**

On my final trip through the city of Isfahan it was clear that the city was in absolute chaos. There were tanks at the intersections of all major roads, armored personnel carriers with mounted machine guns were running through the city, and I could hear occasional gunfire in the distance. The army, still loyal to the Shah, was fighting with idealistic young people who were throwing stones and fire bombs at any military vehicle that passed. Our bus went by two burned out jeeps and a staff car along the evacuation route to the airport. As we left the city I noticed a military road block set up to prevent anyone who might be sympathetic to the Ayatollah's cause from entering the city and adding to the chaos.

The airport was crowded and there was no perceptible order in what was taking place. As frantic passengers were being passed through the security gate and stacked up in the departure area, the Iranian police were searching everyone to make sure that no Iranian cultural items (i.e., money, gold, diamonds and antiquities) were being smuggled out of the country. They were confiscating gold coins, jewelry and money that exceeded some unspecified amount. I didn't have much cash on me so I was safe there; however, I did have eight gold coins in my hand.

Ten Months in Iran

Before I left the house I put the coins in my left hand and then wrapped it with a bandage. I had heard what was taking place at the airport and I wasn't going to loose my gold coins. I took an XACTO knife and jabbed it into the heel of my right hand and blotted the blood on the bandage. I had come to know the Iranians well and I knew that blood was one of the un-clean things they were taught to by their religion to avoid. At the gate when the guard asked to see my hands I thrust my blood stained bandage at him and he immediately backed up, made a sour looking face and waved me through the gate.

There was standing room only in the boarding area where everyone had to fight for the attention of the airline employees. My ticket was for a TWA flight that wasn't due to take off for another two days, but I had received word from Bell that I should go immediately to the airport and get on any available flight and that my ticket would be honored. The customs people were processing departing passengers for awhile but dropped that idea. As the boarding area became packed to capacity, what little organization and process the airlines had managed to maintain began to crumble. Finally an airline employee stood up on a counter and told everyone that they were going to put people on any plane available. He added that everyone should make sure that their bags were properly marked because their bags may well be put on a different plane.

I had a ticket to London but was put on a flight to Istanbul and my luggage was put on a flight to New York. The flight from Isfahan to Istanbul was miserable; there was nothing to drink or eat on board and the flight was packed, they even had passengers sitting in flight attendant jump seats. It was truly the flight from hell; most of the women were crying because the police had taken all of their

Ten Months in Iran

jewelry and all of the children were crying because they were confused, tired, hungry and thirsty.

When I got off the plane in Istanbul I got the feeling that I had escaped from one war zone and landed in another. The airport was an armed camp. There were sandbagged gun emplacements on each side of the terminal doors and machinegun emplacements located in the center and both ends of the building's roof. Two very large tanks were parked at the ends of the terminal and there were flack jacketed soldiers armed with loaded machine guns walking around inside the terminal.

The Istanbul International Airport Terminal was one of the most unimpressive terminals I have ever seen. The building looked like an abandoned warehouse that someone decided to turn into an airport terminal. Walking into the terminal from the plane you found yourself standing in the midst of several tables belonging to the terminal restaurant. I had to walk to one end of the long building to find the ticket counter where I could book a flight to London. After making my flight arrangements, I thought about getting something to eat; however, after looking at the pre-made sandwiches I decided to just have a Coke and potato chips and wait until I got to London to eat. While having my Coke and chips, I read a report in an old English paper I found in the terminal about 200 people being shot and killed in Istanbul during a demonstration in May of the previous year. I was lucky, I was in the terminal only about two hours before I got a flight to London; some of the people I became acquainted with on the flight had to wait an additional ten to twelve hours for their connecting flights. I was just as happy to get out of Turkey as I was getting out of Iran.

During my quiet and quite civilized flight to London on a British airline, I read and edited the notes I had made

Ten Months in Iran

witnessing the clashes between the army and the demonstrators from my roof top observation point.

8:45 PM

The clear-streets curfew has been in effect for forty five minutes. The normal practice of breaking curfew by taunting the soldiers and burning tires in the street has been dampened by an evening shower that just ended. The deserted streets glistened under the street lights and the only motion visible was the flickering reflections of the street lights in puddles rippled by a slight breeze. Our street is quiet but I here the sound of demonstrators from other parts of the city. The rain cooled the evening air down a little and gave it a clean fresh scent.

From my rooftop vantage point I hear what sounds like one person running down the sidewalk. On the corner, I can see a young boy that I would guess is about fifteen years old looking up and down the main street. He crossed the street and disappeared into a dark alley. The fresh clean air left by the rain is being overridden now by the smell of burning tires that's drifting over the city.

9:00 PM

Up the main street to the North I hear chanting: "God is good. God is great." The chanting is being picked up now by the young boys on the corner and I hear it spreading to the East. I see the reflections of the fires now on the smoke that is hanging in the air and on the taller buildings. I hear fast moving vehicles on the main road in front of the university.

The streets are slowly coming alive with people emerging from every shadow and every door. They're mostly young men and boys, all chanting "God is good. God is great." Now they're running up the main street to the North. The street is well lit now by fires set by the demonstrators.

Ten Months in Iran

9:30 PM

I hear shooting from the South (near the river). Single shots are being fired as I climb up on top of the small building covering the stairway to the roof to get a better view. From there I see fires burning everywhere. The single shots are now being followed by automatic rifle fire. I hear people screaming and running. Now I also hear heavy military vehicles coming down the street. There seems to be no effort being made to extinguish the fires. I think some of the fires may have been automobiles because I see large fire balls rising up, followed by loud explosions. I think it may be automobile gas tanks exploding.

10:00 PM

The lights have gone out all over the city. I see and hear what I believe to be 20mm machinegun fire. I also see the red trail of tracers ricocheting off buildings and into the black night sky. A large military truck just stopped at my corner and a squad of soldiers jumped out. They are forming a line across the street from sidewalk to sidewalk and are marching to the North. The smoke from burning tires is hanging heavy in the street now but the fires have gotten dimmer.

10:30 PM

The young men and boys are getting more aggressive, some are throwing rocks at the soldiers. The soldiers are shooting over the heads of the demonstrators trying to get them off the street.

A young man who broke away from the crowd to throw a fire bomb at the soldiers has just been killed. The other demonstrators are chanting: "May God take you to heaven." They chant this over and over three times. I have heard this chant in the distance but could not make out

Ten Months in Iran

what they were saying and didn't know its significance until now.

11:00 PM
A light rain is falling now but it's not dampening the spirit of the demonstrators. They are continuing to torment the soldiers. I see the flashes now and then from fire bombs being thrown in the street.

Another large military truck has stopped at my corner and another squad of soldiers is getting out. They too are forming a line across the street from sidewalk to sidewalk and starting to march to the North. I think the two groups of soldiers are going to try to box-in the demonstrators on the main street. Lots of screaming and chanting going on but I can't tell what is being said.

11:30 PM
As the soldiers close the trap on the remaining demonstrators, the ones that had escaped are reappearing to the North and South of the soldiers. Now the soldiers are effectively divided into two small groups with demonstrators surrounding them. The demonstrators are not aggressively attacking the soldiers, nor are they stoning them. However, their political and obscene chanting is increasing in tempo and an occasional stone is thrown.

The two groups of soldiers moved to the East side of the street and then worked their way along the buildings to re-group. Once together, they separated and started moving the demonstrators off the main street to the north and south. The demonstrators are now breaking car windows and setting them on fire. I hear shots being fired and then the chant "May God take you to heaven." I can only believe that another demonstrator has died.

12

Ten Months in Iran

12:00 PM
The demonstrations must be much worse on the other side of the river because I still see the occasional 20mm tracer zip off through the dark sky and the fires are much worse than on our main street because sky is glowing from the fires.

My street is quiet now. I hear a military truck coming; it has a spot light on it and they are picking up the dead bodies from the street. I hear the truck move and stop, then the thump of a body being thrown onto the truck bed. I watch as they load the three bodies that are visible from my vantage point. One soldier picked up the feet and the other soldier took hold of the arms, then they swung the body back and fourth a couple of times until they thought it had enough momentum to make it into the truck. As the truck went down our main street I heard it stop two more times. Each stop was punctuated with the now familiar thump of the body hitting the truck bed.

12:15 PM
The trucks have gone and everything is quiet.
There are no more rifle shots, no vehicles moving and no fires.
I think Isfahan has gone to sleep for the night.

Tim, my roommate, went to the roof with me tonight and as we watched and listened to the action on the street we failed to notice that a soldier had taken up position just inside our street on the corner. Tonight was a night when the gunfights were heaver than usual. Tim was busy copying down all the chants that he heard. We heard a few single shots being fired down the street and it didn't sound too far away. Then, the soldier on the corner opened up with his automatic rifle and fired off five or six quick rounds. I turned to tell Tim that I hadn't even seen the soldier on the corner and to my surprise he was laying

Ten Months in Iran

on the roof. I asked him what he was doing and he told me that that is what they always do in the movies. I looked down at him in disbelief and told him to "get up here". He got up, brushed himself off and looked at me with a sheepish grin. I don't think you have to worry about getting shot up here, I said, there isn't any reason for him to shoot in this direction. We're on a dead end alley where there aren't any demonstrators; that's why he picked this alley and has his back to it. Besides, if you hear a shot, it's already gone; you never hear the one that gets you. He continued to copy the chants and some of them weren't too religious:

```
God is good, God is great!
Liberty, freedom, Islamic government!
Welcome Khomeini, we don't want the
Shah!
Who carried away the oil?    America!
Who carried away the gas?    Russia!
Who carried away the money? Pahlavi!
Death to the Pahlavi Dynasty!
Carter said "I want Farah's pussy."
The Shah said "I'll give you oil as her
dowry."
```

After the action stopped, I went downstairs and found that Tim had candles burning all over the house. He said he didn't like the dark and was afraid that one of the demonstrators would break in through the roof. I told him that everything was quiet now and that he could put the candles out and go to bed.

Ten Months in Iran

Chapter 1
Isfahan, Iran

I arrived in Isfahan early in the summer of 1978. After landing we were made to wait inside the plane for nearly forty minutes with the engines off and the doors open to allow any breeze that might be blowing to flow through the hot plane. It was unbearably hot, uncomfortable and the smell of 180 sweaty bodies was starting to induce nausea. We were told to remain in our seats and that the toilets wouldn't operate while the engines were off. The degree of absurdity in making passengers wait inside an plane, with the engines off, when the outside air temperature is over one hundred degrees is only surpassed by the degree of stupidity possessed by the person responsible for approving such an action. This event turned out to be a harbinger of my future experiences with Iranian Shiite Muslims and the absurdity of their interpretation of Islam.

Passengers who had small children were having an extremely difficult time controlling them and keeping them quiet and in their seats. One of the young female Iranian flight attendants took pity on those mothers who had small children and on the older passengers who were starting to look a little flushed and gave them cold drinks. The flight attendants were not doing much better than the

Ten Months in Iran

passengers because you could see the perspiration soaking through their uniforms. The male attendants had taken off their jackets and their shirts were soaking wet with sweat. It was the most miserable experience I've ever had on a commercial plane and what I didn't know was that the situation was only going to get worse.

As I stepped off the plane, I knew I was somewhere quite unlike anyplace I'd ever been. We didn't get off and walk through the ubiquitous retractable walkway that connects an arriving plane to an air-conditioned terminal. We were told to exit at least a quarter mile from the terminal and made to stand on the hot tarmac in the sun with an air temperature that exceeded 100^0 F. We had to wait for the bags to be unloaded and then we had to find and get our own bags from the pile of two hundred or more piled on the tarmac. I helped a British lady who had two small children, three carry-on bags and a forlorn look of malady on her face that I was sure preceded hysteria. I found her five bags and my two and placed them together on the tarmac; then we waited for a bus to take us and our bags to the terminal. It took one hour and thirty minutes to get inside the terminal. Once inside, our bags were ripped apart, we were searched and our passports seized. We had to fill out forms indicating who we were, who we worked for, where we were going to stay while in Isfahan and how long we intended to stay. We were told that we would get our passports back in three to four weeks. Of all the countries I visited during twenty years of traveling, Iran was the only country that didn't stamp my passport and hand it back to me on the spot; even in China, the agent looked at me, looked at my passport, stamped my passport and handed it back to me.

I continued to help the lady who had the two small children and eight bags during the two hours and several moves that it took to get through customs and

Ten Months in Iran

immigration. My helping her caused us a little problem because the immigration officer thought I was her husband and he wanted to know why we had different names. We had a hell of a time convincing him that I was not married to her and that I was only helping her because she needed help. Once on the other side of the restricted area I tried to pass her bags off to her Iranian husband but he refused to take hold of any of them and immediately started giving her hell for allowing me to help her and wanting to know where we had met and how long she had known me. At that point I was sorry that I had helped her, seeing the additional trouble it had gotten her into. As I was leaving the area, I looked back and he was still giving her hell and still hadn't picked up either of the children or any of the bags. Well, honey, I thought, you married him. After I finally got out of there I was directed to an airport bus parked outside the terminal. During the bus ride to the hotel in downtown Isfahan I thought about the indoctrination course that was designed and delivered by Bell Helicopter to prepare Americans for the shock of being dropped into Iranian culture. The indoctrination course wasn't adequate and I don't think any course could be. With the exception of the overpowering smell of fermenting body sweat that permeated this bus, the ride was reminiscent of the suicide bus rides I had been on from Bangkok to Lop Buri in Thailand; so, I did the same thing in Iran that I did in Thailand; I closed my eyes and tried to think about something more pleasant.

My first impression of Isfahan was that everything was brown, tan or gray. The buildings, streets, sidewalks and cars were brown, tan or gray. The only relief you got from this tricolor world was if you were lucky enough to be around some trees or grass. Outside of the public parks, grass was scarce in Isfahan; however, many of the streets in the city were lined with trees. We were told the traffic in Isfahan was hectic and that most drivers didn't pay

Ten Months in Iran

attention to traffic laws. That turned out to be the most understated warning of the entire indoctrination course. During the bus ride to the hotel, and later by riding in taxies, I learned that Iranian drivers only paid attention to a stop light if a policeman was standing under it and that stop signs were not to be obeyed at any time for any reason. The rule seemed to be whomever got to the intersection first, or had the loudest horn, had the right-of-way.

They warned us in the indoctrination course in Texas that several Americans had been injured and a few killed while trying to cross one-way streets because they had only looked one way before crossing. They also told us to always look both ways on one-way streets because one-way streets were only one-way if all lanes were full. They told us it was perfectly acceptable for an Iranian driver to go down a one-way street (the wrong way) on the sidewalk if all the lanes were full. Traffic circles had similar unwritten rules; a traffic circle had to be used as a traffic circle if you were going less than ¾ the way around. If you had to go ¾ the way around, you could take the short cut and go the wrong way for ¼ of the circle on the outside lane or, if the circle was full, use the sidewalk. The city buses were the real killers; a city bus was free to go down any one-way street the wrong way at any time, even if the street was full, the cars were obligated to get out of the way. However, the true free-spirits of the road in Iran were the people on motorcycles and motorbikes because they were not obligated to follow any traffic rules at any time. They didn't have to stop for a traffic signal even if a police officer was standing under the light, but they did always try to do it behind his back.

The airport bus delivered me to the Kourosh International Hotel in downtown Isfahan. I've stayed at beautiful hotels

Ten Months in Iran

in Paris, London, Munich and Rome; however, none of them can compare with the elegant decorum of the Kourosh. The furniture in my eighth floor two room apartment was white lacquer and white lacquer with gold-leaf trim; the upholstery was a royal-blue silk. I felt like I was living in a king's palace. The Kourosh provided almost everything an American could ask for when living away from home. The top floor had a nightclub that had good food, good drinks and good music. The ground floor had stores that provided most of the items that you would run out of if you stayed very long. Entering into the hotel at the end of the day was like escaping from Iran and entering a never-never land where you could eat American, Italian, French or Chinese food or go to the nightclub for a drink.

The Kourosh was mostly full of Americans, English, French, Germans and Italians because most of the Russians, Iranians, Turks, Greeks, Syrians, Lebanese and Iraqis stayed at cheaper hotels. I could generally tell where someone was from by listening to them talk because, even if you don't understand their language, you get to the point where you can identify the sound of a particular language or a language group like Slavic, Germanic or Semitic. I could not understand Farsi; however, I got to the point where I could tell if an Iranian was from Teheran or the countryside. But, I must admit that I was stumped many times by languages I heard in the lobby of the Kourosh hotel.

While staying at the hotel, I met Tim Brown an American language specialist who was employed by Bell Helicopter to teach Iranian soldiers to use an eight-hundred-word vocabulary in English. Tim was a mousy sort of guy (I think he may have been gay) but his intelligence was over the top. He spoke Farsi, French, Russian and Italian. Tim and I quickly became good friends; first, I think, because

Ten Months in Iran

we arrived in Isfahan at the same time and second, I think, being with me gave him a feeling of security during his first few days in the city. He knew that in addition to being a helicopter pilot that I was also an ex-Green Beret. During our first few days in Isfahan he was constantly after me to go with him to explore the city; I also needed to become familiar with the city, so I usually went with him.

The shaft for the two main elevators in the hotel came down into the middle of the lobby, so when the elevator doors opened you were facing the front doors of the hotel. The hotel restaurant was located about twenty feet behind the elevator shaft, and if you were coming down to the restaurant you could either turn right or left out of the elevator and walk directly into the restaurant.

During my first week at the hotel I stepped out of the elevator one evening, made a hard right turn for the restaurant and ran my face into the perfumed breasts of a very tall woman who was making a left turn into the elevator. Each of her breasts was as big as a melon and I bounced off them. I am five foot nine inches tall, with my shoes on, and my nose was even with the nipples of her breasts. After regaining my senses, I looked up at her and laughed; she looked down at me and laughed. I told her that I was sorry and she said something to me, with a very big smile on her face, in a language that I could not identify and continued on her way. She was the biggest most beautiful woman I had ever seen and I couldn't talk to her. Although I continued to look for her during my stay at the hotel, I never saw her again.

The next day at breakfast I was telling Tim about her but I was sure he thought I was making it up. As we sat waiting for service, Tim identified seventeen languages being spoken just at the tables that were close enough to us that he could hear what was being said. I was never very

Ten Months in Iran

adventurous for breakfast at the hotel because I knew the cooks were hired off the street and not professional chefs like the club restaurant on the top floor. To be safe, I normally got eggs, bacon and toast because it's hard to screw up eggs, bacon and toast. So, when the waiter stopped at our table and asked what we wanted, I placed my usual ordered and got the reply "no bacon".

"You don't have any bacon?" I said.

"Yes, we have bacon, but can't serve bacon."

For a short while, talking with this waiter made me feel like I was on *Candid Camera*.

"You have bacon." I said.

"Yes, we have bacon." He said.

"But, I can't get bacon?"

"Yes, no bacon."

This would probably have been very irritating to someone who didn't have the warped and exaggerated sense of humor I inherited from my mother; but, to me it was so funny that I started laughing. One of the other waiters came over, one who had waited on me before and knew me, and asked what was wrong. I told him the story and he told me that my water was new and that his English wasn't very good yet. He told me the reason I couldn't get any bacon that morning was because the bacon cook didn't show up for work.

"The bacon cook." I said. "You have a cook just for the bacon?"

"Yes," he said. "All of the regular cooks in the kitchen are Muslims and they will not touch bacon. The bacon cook is a Filipino and he didn't show up for work this morning."

I looked at the waiter who was still standing there and told him, scrambled eggs and toast. The no-bacon thing never happened again, so I think they must have hired two bacon cooks.

21

Ten Months in Iran

The Iranians are very class conscious and it was evident in the hotel restaurant for breakfast more than any other place or time. As far as I could figure out, the pecking order in the workforce went something like this from top to bottom: Koreans, Filipinos, Afghans, Indians and last Bangladeshis. The Koreans and Filipinos were cooks and waiters; the Afghans were waiters; the Indians and Bangladeshis, who were actually in the same bag, were assigned the most menial jobs and the dirtiest jobs.

The Iranians also seem very class conscious when it cames to their paying customers; that order from top to bottom went like this: Americans (I think because we gave bigger tips), English and Canadians, Europeans, Russians, Koreans, Filipinos, Afghans, Indians and Bangladeshis. There were many nationalities there that I couldn't identify but as a general rule the darker the skin the lower they were on the list, except for black Americans and as far as I could tell they were treated just like the white Americans.

Probing for the Truth

Tim had a T-shirt that had "Thank God It's Friday" printed on it in Russian. During the six weeks we had to spend at the hotel before we found a house, he would wear the shirt on a weekend, pretend to be Russian, and go for taxi rides. Once in the taxi he would ask the driver, in Russian if the driver spoke Russian, what he thought about the Americans. The next weekend he would wear an American T-shirt and do the same thing in English and ask the driver what he thought about the Russians. The results were easy to predict; whatever nationality he pretended to be, that's who the driver loved and detested the other. On some weekends he would pretend to be Italian and the driver would hate the Russians, French and the Americans. The only consensus that he was ever able

Ten Months in Iran

to come up with was that the Iranian taxi drivers always liked the Italians and always hated the French.

Our House in Isfahan

Tim and I rented a house in an affluent neighborhood across the street from the University of Isfahan. During the time we lived together I don't think we saw each other more than three or four times a week because he worked at night and I worked during the day. He had the car we leased at night and I had the car during the day; on weekends we either took turns or we went someplace together. He liked going to the bazaar and he also liked visiting historical sites. He loved to play Scrabble with anyone but me; and that's because I was not a challenge to him whatsoever, even when he helped me. You can't play scrabble with someone who can speak five languages and be a challenge, let alone expect to win. Mentally he was a giant; physically he was a lightweight, maybe 115 pounds and five foot eight inches tall. I often wondered where he gathered the courage to go to Iran to teach.

Our landlord was an unassuming quiet sort of man whom I only saw three times while we were in the house. I saw him when we rented the house, another time when he had some plumbing work done and when we left the house to return to the states. He was an older man and had lived in the house himself until he learned he could rent it to Americans for twice what it would cost him to rent a house himself. So, he rented us his house and he rented another house and made about five hundred dollars a month profit.

The house was one of six single-story houses connected together side-by-side along an alley off the main street leading to the university. For me, living within the city limits of Isfahan was quite confining. All a passerby could

23

Ten Months in Iran

see while walking down my street was an eight foot wall on each side of the street. Each house on my street had a twenty foot by forty foot courtyard that was bordered on three sides by eight-foot high walls. The wall facing the street joined with all the other courtyard walls to form an eight foot wall that ran the length of our street. Each courtyard had two access doors, one for foot traffic and one for an automobile. The other side of the street was exactly the same except that one lot had a two story house and one lot was vacant.

Being inside the house was like being in a fort and unless your neighbor was on his roof no one could see what was going on in your courtyard. My courtyard was paved except for a persimmon tree and an eight foot diameter pond complete with fish. For an American boy who was used to looking down the street and seeing the grassy yards of twenty or more houses, it was like living in a concrete box. There were no windows in the house; only a set of sliding glass double doors for each room that faced the courtyard. The back wall of my house was the back wall of another house to my rear and the side walls of my house were the side walls of my neighbor's houses.

The only way you could see anything or get some air was to go up on the roof. Access to the roof was by a steep stairway that led to a phone-booth like structure on the roof. The interior of the house was typical Iranian; the same tile that covered the floor ran three feet up every wall making the room look amazingly like a three foot deep swimming pool, except for the fact that one end had sliding glass doors. The one thing I really did like about the house was that it was easy to clean. On cleaning day I would move all the furniture from one room into the adjoining room, drag the garden hose in, hose down the entire room and then squeegee the water out the door into

Ten Months in Iran

the courtyard. Then I would repeat the procedure in the adjoining room.

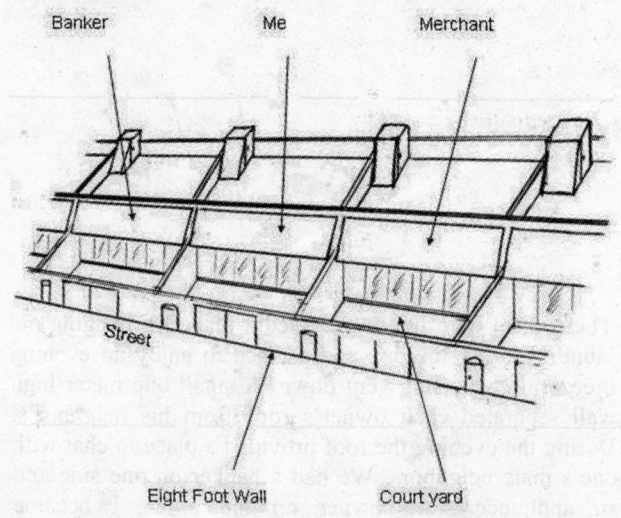

Banker — Me — Merchant

Street

Eight Foot Wall — Court yard

The house had two toilets, one western toilet and one Iranian toilet. The western toilet, inside the house, was actually an Iranian toilet with a western commode anchored over the hole. The Iranian toilet was in a little house in the courtyard and only offered the standard cavity in the floor accompanied by two skid pads for your feet and a small hose for washing yourself (Iranians and Arabs don't use toilet paper).

Ten Months in Iran

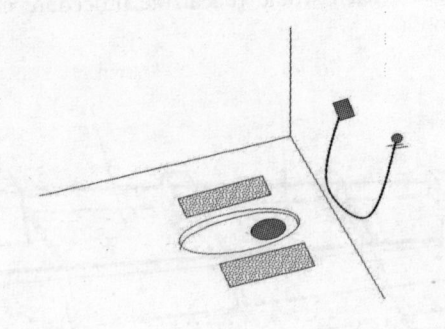

The roof of each house provided a place for hanging out laundry during the day and a place to enjoy an evening breeze after the sun went down. A small one meter high wall separated each owner's roof from his neighbor's. During the evening the roof provided a place to chat with one's male neighbors. We had a banker on one side and an appliance store owner on the other. I became acquainted with each of these men and, over time, with the wife and children of the banker.

The banker was about fifty years old, five foot ten inches tall, a little overweight at 200 pounds, no beard, educated in the United States and always dressed in a well-made Western suit; he impressed me as being very conservative because he always kept to non-political and non-religious subjects when we talked. When the Ayatollah was so much on everyone's mind that it had to be mentioned, his only comment was that he believed that the Ayatollah would do the right thing. His children, ages ten and twelve, were in grade school but spoke English relatively well. I had no problem talking with them. I found out from Tim that during days when they didn't have to go to school that they would come over and practice their French with him.

Ten Months in Iran

They knew that I had been all over the world, so when they started studying world geography I gave them a list of the countries I had been in and they would interview me when one of those countries came up as a topic in school. They thought it was so neat to talk to someone who had actually been to the places they were studying. When the United States came up for study I thought they were going to drag me to school with them. They went much deeper into world geography than we did when I was in school; I remember because I always liked geography and history and wanted to know more than just the date that something happened. I must have been very irritating to my school teachers because I was always asking why. They would say something like "the Norman conquest of Saxon England took place between 1066 and 1072" and I would ask why did the Normans, who had the area that is now France, want England? I was told more than once in high school in Newark, Ohio to be quiet and just remember the date because I didn't need to know why. So, when the bankers children would ask me why, I always did my best to give them an answer. Their mother was intent on getting her boys out of the country and into a school in either France or the United States.

I was given a puppy that a friend's daughter had rescued from the street but couldn't keep where she was living. I named the dog Lucky because if she hadn't picked it up it would've died or been killed within a few days. Most Iranians don't like dogs; consequently, most children in Iran never have the pleasure of loving and playing with a dog. The banker's children fell in love with Lucky and played with him whenever they got the opportunity. They would watch for me to come down the alley in the evening and run to meet me. I'd let them into my courtyard and they would play with Lucky until their mother called for them to come home. These children had

Ten Months in Iran

not yet been exposed to the Iranian idea that dogs were possessed by the devil and, I suspect, their father would never tell them.

The banker's wife was about forty-five years old and a big lady, about six feet tall and about 170 pounds. However, she was a very lovely and feminine lady. She had typical Iranian black hair, dark eyes and a beautiful complexion. I would see her occasionally hanging out laundry; she liked to talk with me to practice her English and I found out that she also liked to practice her French with Tim. She told me that she had met her husband while attending college in the states. She majored in physics with a math minor but couldn't find a job after returning to Iran so she just stayed home and took care of the house and tutored the children. She was much more vocal about what she believed than her husband was. She believed the return if the Ayatollah would be a disaster for the country. In fact, she referred to the Ayatollah as an undereducated social parasite. I often thought her inability to get a teaching job was due to the fact that she was too educated, too liberal and too Westernized even for the liberal academic crowd. I never saw her in a chador[1]; she always had red lipstick on and was dressed in smartly styled Western clothing.

The merchant was a short stocky man about five foot five and 175 pounds. I guessed his age to be around sixty but he was in very good shape. He was from a well-to-do family and was educated in Iran where he majored in business administration. You had only to talk with him a short while to realize that he was rich and intelligent; he spoke excellent English, had strong opinions about everything and wasn't afraid to express them. One

---

[1] Chador – The black garment that covers an Iranian woman from head to toe. However, Iranian women do not cover their faces.

Ten Months in Iran

evening when a nice cool breeze was blowing across the roof, we had a long talk; a talk that was to be the beginning of my continuing education about the Shiites, Islam and Iranian culture, because this neighbor loved to talk. I never saw a woman at his house so I thought he wasn't married; however, when I asked him why he wasn't married all he did was give me a big, deep, long laugh. I asked him why that question was so funny. It's funny he said because I have three wives. So I asked him why I had never seen any of them.

That's when he started telling me about his philosophy of life and what it took to make multiple marriages work. He told me the first thing he learned when he took his second wife was that you can't have two women in the same house. Then I asked him how he could stand having three wives. He explained to me that he'd placed each wife in her own house in separate sections of the city. I still didn't quite grasp the situation and asked him again why I'd never seen any of them. He told me they weren't allowed at this house; this was his private place to be alone and that his wives didn't even know his address. Any time I had a question about an Iranian custom or about Islam, he would do his best to give me an answer I could understand.

One Friday I saw a man dressed in a white one-piece garment crawling along the street; he looked as though he had been rolled around in a coal-dust bin. His knees were bleeding and the front of the garment was blood stained. I could tell by the look of the garment that it had been clean a short time before this activity had started. Except where the soil had been applied, it was white, not gray. As soon as people saw him they would turn away and not look back. I couldn't wait to get home and ask my neighbor what this was all about. This was one of the few times he told me "I have no idea how to explain that to you." I guess there are some things that can't be translated. I

Ten Months in Iran

enjoyed my talks with him and always thought he should write a book on how to be happy because he was the happiest and most contented person I ever met in Iran. He was always in a good mood.

Buying Food

It took a little time for me to catch onto the secret of knowing when and where to buy things in Isfahan. There were official government stores and there were local indigenous stores to choose from. The government stores had a wide variety of imported items but they weren't cheap; the local stores had locally manufactured and produced items that were priced reasonably plus occasional black market items that weren't priced reasonably but they were available for purchase. The trick to getting what you wanted was in knowing when the stores got their deliveries because most of the desirable items were gone the first day on the shelf, whether it was a government store or a local store. Food, in general, was never a problem; the problem was with specialty items like good cheese, Spanish olives, American style bread and coffee. The government store eventually got a reasonable facsimile of American toilet paper; however, it was gone as soon as they put it on the shelf. The government store would also get a one-time-only shipment of an item (such a razor blades or deodorant) so it was good to get to know the manager of the store so you could be aware of special items being delivered. Tim was especially good at this task since he spoke fluent Farsi and loved to talk to anyone who would talk to him.

The government store was pretty much like an American supermarket. It was big, brightly lit and clean. The aisles were stocked with food and although some items sold out, the shelves were never empty. The local food stores were

Ten Months in Iran

just smaller versions of the government store in that they were well lit and clean. The local stores usually didn't sell out of items as quickly as the government store. Shopping was generally a pleasant experience and the stores were never crowded. You almost never saw an Iranian woman in the stores; the men did the shopping. The women you did see there were American and European women shopping for their families. You did not stock up large quantities of food in Iran. Shopping was more in the manner of the Europeans, you either bought today what you were going to eat today or you bought food for the next two or three days if you had a good refrigerator and you lived in an area where the electricity didn't go off too frequently. The electricity in my neighborhood under normal conditions went off at least once a week and was off for as long as three hours.

Making a Long Distance Call

Placing a long distance call in Iran was another unique experience. We didn't have a phone for the house yet so the only way to make a call was from the central office. It was more difficult to place a call to the United States from Iran than it was from the war zone in Vietnam. To make a call to my mother I had to make an appointment, days in advance, at the main telephone exchange office in Isfahan. I had to tell them who I was going to call, where they were located and what the number was. Then I had to show up at the telephone exchange at the appointed time, check in at the desk and sit down to wait for an open line. After about thirty minutes of waiting, I was directed to one of the twenty booths lining the hallway.

Calls to the United States weren't cheap. My ten-minute call cost about thirty dollars. However, I did get to hear mom's and dad's voices and thank them for the care packages they were sending to me. A friend of mine who

Ten Months in Iran

worked in security told me to be careful when making a call to another country because all calls were either listened to live or recorded and listened to later. I didn't care because I didn't have anything to hide, but I could see where it would be of concern if you had to talk about family matters that you didn't want the world to know about. I used this method three or four times to call home before we got the phone in our house.

Conducting Business in Iran

I soon found out that if you conducted any type of business in Iran, you had to pay someone a bribe. My first exposure to this hidden tax was when we went to get a telephone. At first the phone company said it was impossible to get a phone in Isfahan. But, if I would give him some money he might be able to 'pay someone else' to see if they could give me some type of priority. I gave him the equivalent of five dollars and he gave me a name and the office location where I should go. The next man I talked to said that he could get me moved up on the list but he would have to 'pay someone else' to do it. Once again it cost me five dollars and the man left the room for a short while. When he came back he said that I was on the top of the list but that he couldn't give the installers the order to install the phone; that order had to come from another department. So, I was off again to pay another bribe. Finally I was in the office of the man who could give the order to install the phone. I figured since he was such an important person I should give him a bigger bribe so I gave him ten dollars. My phone was installed the next day after I paid the installer who claimed he didn't have enough time left in his work day to do the job.

My second exposure to this hidden tax was after the landlord had some work done on the plumbing and I was

Ten Months in Iran

informed by the workman that it would take two or three days for an inspector to come around and inspect his work. And, until it was inspected, the water could not be turned back on. I suggested to him that certainly he knew someone who could get the work inspected sooner. He told me that he might be able to get someone to come if I were willing to pay for the extra time he would have to work. I gave him twenty American dollars and asked him to see what he could do. He got the inspection completed within hours and an additional five dollars got the water turned on at the same time.

The third time was when Tim leased a jeep and I needed to get a permit to drive. The person at the state office said that it would take a few weeks to get all my papers checked and the forms completed since I didn't have my passport. So, one more time I started suggesting that he probably knew someone who could get it done sooner if he really tried. And, once again we went through the process. It took thirty American dollars to get me a permit within four hours.

I figured out that bribes in Iran ranged from 100% to 200% of the normal cost of whatever business you're trying to conduct. When I shipped an Oriental rug to my mother in the United States the normal shipping cost was thirty dollars. Then it took another thirty dollars to make sure that the rug would get past exit customs. I think the only reason that I didn't have to pay a bribe to get my incoming mail was that it came to me through Bell Helicopter's company mail system and not through the Iranian mail system.

Ten Months in Iran
Banking in Isfahan

Inflation was rampant in Iran and since all Bell Helicopter employees were paid in Iranian Rials it was a good idea to buy a good stable foreign currency if you were going to keep much cash on hand. The American dollar wasn't doing all that well at the time, so I always exchanged my Rials for German Marks. Going to the bank in Isfahan was a unique experience and not something to be attempted if you were in a hurry. The two banks that I dealt with in Isfahan had very small offices.

When you entered the bank you were automatically in line along the left wall; the twenty foot long queue was separated from the lobby by a short three foot high wall. After making your way through the queue you made a right-hand turn into the narrow four foot wide lobby that was as long as the queue. There were normally three tellers on duty. The teller area was also about four foot wide and twenty feet long. So, the whole visible office was about ten feet wide and twenty feet long. There was a door behind the tellers but I never knew what was on the other side of that door. I suspect it was a storage room.

I could never see what the young lady was doing behind the five foot high counter that separated the tellers from the customers but, due to the fact that it took such an unreasonably long time to conduct any transaction, I always suspected that she was using a stylus to record all my transactions on a clay tablet. Changing my Rials for Marks took around twenty minutes every time. I bought American Express Traveler's Checks one time; after that one time I made a promise to myself that I would never again under any circumstances do it again. I finally got so tired of waiting for her to complete whatever it was she was doing that I asked about the delay. She told me that she had to record all the numbers of the checks

Ten Months in Iran

individually and to whom they were issued. She said she couldn't record checks 001 through 050. I wanted so much to ask her if she was recording the numbers on a clay tablet but decided against it because I was sure it would only cause additional delay.

After I started accumulating a lot of money I decided I needed to condense my holding into something more manageable so I went to the bank and purchased eight gold coins at $300 each. The gold coins were easier to hide than 6,000.00 DM[2] in cash, especially since the highest denomination I could get was 100 DM. Another absolutely maddening thing about banking in Iran was trying to figure out what day the bank was going to be open and then what time it was going to be open on that particular day. Had I been able to read Farsi my life, as far a banking was concerned, would have been much simpler.

The Wedding Party

One evening as the merchant and I stood on the roof talking, I noticed what looked like a party going on in the courtyard across the street. I told my neighbor that it didn't look like much of a party because it was only a group of men and they were all standing around like it was a wake.

"Watch the window on the second floor." He said.

"What am I looking for?"

"Just watch the window."

It wasn't long before the window was opened and a man in a white gown threw a white cloth to the courtyard. All the men cheered as one man picked up the cloth and waved it over his head as he danced around the courtyard.

"Ok," I said, "what's going on over there?"

---

[2] German Marks

Ten Months in Iran

"You have just witnessed the successful consummation of a marriage. An Iranian bride is expected to be a virgin and therefore, to bleed like a stuck pig on her wedding night as proof that she was a virgin. The male family members and guests of the groom wait in the courtyard below the bedroom window to see proof of this in the form of a blood soaked cloth thrown from the window after the bride has been deflowered. The groom's father, brother or uncle picks up the blood soaked cloth and waves it around to show everyone that the groom has performed his duty and did indeed marry a virgin. If the couple has had sex before being married, and he still thinks enough of her to marry her, the groom will kill a cat and soak the cloth with the cat's blood. This covers up the sins of the bride and allows the groom to hold her up as a trophy before his family."

"Oh," I said. "That's primitive."

"Yes," he said. "It is. Most Iranians have dropped the practice but some old families are hanging onto the custom."

"I've always believed that virginity was highly overrated." I said.

"I think the origin of the custom can be traced to rich people who were worried about who was going to inherit their money and carry on the family name. I also think poor people picked up the custom because it was free and it was something they could do to mimic the rich," he said.

"So," I said. "That's the climax of the wedding ceremony?"

"I'm afraid so, they'll all go home now."

A Day of Sightseeing

Tim and I had talked for some time about taking an entire day and visiting historical sites around the city; so, when I

Ten Months in Iran

got home one Friday evening and he presented me with his map and sight seeing itinerary for the next day, I agreed. He had planned the day starting with breakfast at the Kourosh hotel, lunch at the Korean restaurant and back to the Kourosh for supper. After breakfast we planned to spend the morning in the Royal Square located in the center of the city north of the river. The Royal Square was surrounded by the Great Bazaar to the north, the Shah's Mosque to the south, the Sheikh Lotfollah Mosque to the east and the Ali Qapu Palace to the west (see map below).

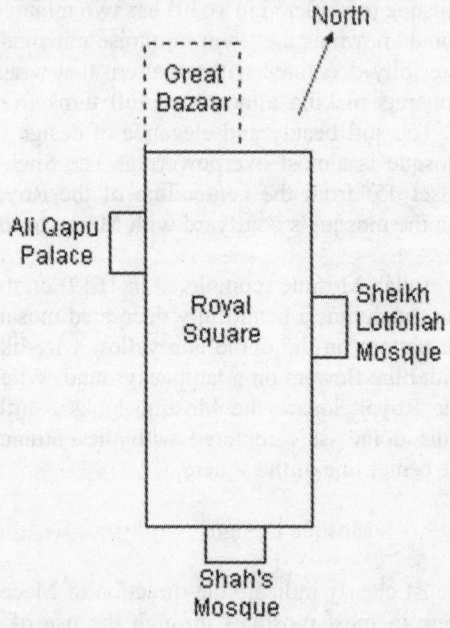

```
                    North ↗

        ┌ ─ ─ ─ ─ ─ ┐
        │   Great   │
        │  Bazaar   │
        └ ─ ─ ─ ─ ─ ┘
   ┌──┐
   │Ali Qapu│
   │Palace  │                    ┌────────┐
   └──┘                          │ Sheikh │
        │   Royal   │            │Lotfollah│
        │  Square   │            │ Mosque │
                                 └────────┘


              ┌──────┐
              │Shah's│
              │Mosque│
              └──────┘
```

In the distant past, public executions were held in the Royal Square and were witnessed by the reigning Shah from the balcony of the Ali Qapu palace (completed in 1590). In more recent times the Shah watched polo

37

Ten Months in Iran

matches from the balcony. The Square is surrounded by four walls that are divided into arcades. The arcades are populated by vendors and you can buy anything from handmade brass platters decorated with intricate geometric designs to common mass-produced souvenirs to food. The Iranian craftsmen are masters at creating a seemingly infinite number of unique geometric patterns for decorating everything from plates to buildings.

The buildings around the square are covered with light blue, dark blue, green, yellow and turquoise mosaic tilework arranged to present floral and geometric patterns. The Shah's Mosque (completed in 1630) has two minarets that have become known as the 'twin turquoise minarets'. They are masterfully decorated with a pattern that wraps around the minarets making almost two full turns from bottom to top. The soft beauty and elegance of design of the Shah's Mosque is almost overpowering. The Shah's Mosque is offset 45^0 from the center line of the Royal Square to align the mosque's courtyard with Mecca to the southwest.

The Sheikh Lotfollah Mosque (completed in 1619) on the east side of the square has a beautifully decorated mosaic tile dome. The pattern on the dome is a yellow wire-like scroll work with blue flowers on a tan background. When standing in the Royal Square the Mosque looks a little odd because the dome isn't centered with the entrance doorway or the center line of the square.

Mosque Design

All mosques must clearly indicate the direction of Mecca and this is done in most mosques through the use of a *mihrab*. A *mihrab* is usually a semicircular recess placed in the wall that faces Mecca. The *mihrab* is usually made from marble or some other stone and may be four to five feet high and two to three feet across the opening. The

Ten Months in Iran

wall that the *mihrab* is placed in may not have any doors or other openings. When entering a mosque you must remove your shoes and step in with your right foot first. You must be clean when entering a mosque and if it is the Friday prayer you are expected to be dressed in good clothes and perfumed.

Women are not restricted from entering a mosque by the Qur'an; however, women entering mosques are not welcomed by the men. In many areas mosques have been closed to women altogether. In those places women can pray only in their homes. This gives the men a sense of superiority because the *Sunna* (the Law taken from the Qur'an and Islamic custom) states that a prayer in a mosque is 25 times more effective than one given in the home.

The Great Bazaar

The Bazaar was a fascinating place. Walking through the bazaar was like walking through time. You could see craftsman making pots, pans, plates and other household articles the same way they were being made hundreds of years ago. You could see blacksmiths making fancy trimmings for houses, tools, ironwork security bars and gates for homes. There were cobblers who would measure your feet today and have handmade shoes ready for you in two days. The tailor would provide you with a similar service.

The whole place was an adventure for the nose too. As you walked along you could smell new leather, newly-dyed cloth, metal being melted, charcoal fires, food of all types and the best smelling place of all, the herb shop. It had dried limes, lemons, parsley, dill, mint, garlic, tarragon, chives and other herbs I couldn't identify. The herb shop had bushels of each herb open in the shop and people purchased pounds of the herbs not just a few

Ten Months in Iran

ounces. I found out that the Iranians eat herbs like we eat celery or carrots. They don't just use them to flavor food, they are the food.

If you had enough money and could speak the right language you could find and purchase anything you wanted at the bazaar. The Russians were constant customers of the bazaar because they would haggle over the price of an item they wanted until the merchant got tired and would sell it to them at their price just to get them out of his shop. The bazaar was like dying and going to heaven for a person who loves antiques. If you took your time and searched every shop you could find things that were not available anywhere else. But, you had to be skillful enough to recognize and pick out the real antiques from all the items that were made to look like they were antiques. I spent days in the bazaar looking for old American coins. They had coins that were more than one hundred years old that were in good shape and sold them for a fraction of what you would pay for them in the states.

Russians in the Bazaar

Tim spoke Russian so well that the Russians we met in the bazaar not only thought he was Russian they thought he was from Moscow. He was able to talk to them about Russia and Moscow because he attended the University of Moscow for a year to study Russian history and language. He understood the Russian psychic. He not only knew what they thought was funny but why they thought it was funny. He knew the jokes they made about the Iranians and when to bring one up during a conversation. He would have been an excellent spy.
It was so funny to watch their reactions when he suddenly stopped speaking Russian with them and said something

Ten Months in Iran

to me in English. It was like he'd thrown ice water on them; they immediately stopped talking and quickly walked away without looking back. Their faces would turn pale and you could see a sudden fear in their eyes.

I found out later from a CIA officer at the United States embassy that the Russians had a large number of business men, engineers, scientists, construction workers and spies in Isfahan. I knew he was with the CIA as soon as he told me his embassy title. Every person I had ever met with that title was an agent for the CIA.

Tim and I spent so much of our day at the palace, mosques, bazaar and food shops around the Royal Square that we just went back to the house to rest up for supper at the Kourosh.

Tim introduced me to Frank and Priscilla Swick as we were having supper. He told me they were ground-school[3] instructors and that they sometimes worked at night to help students who were falling behind in their work. They had been in Isfahan for sixteen months but were planning on going home at the end of their second year. They joined Tim and me at our table and we spent about an hour talking.

Frank was about six foot tall and reasonably well built for a fifty year old man. He had a full head of dark brown hair that was slightly gray around the temples. I found his New York accent even more irritating than normal and I think it was due to the fact that his attitude somehow caused it to seem amplified or exaggerated. Frank truly thought that he was God's gift to the women of the world and that idea was present and evident in everything he said or did. He was always overdressed for the occasion, he was always too aggressive with women and he always wore too much

---

[3] subjects required to support the physical activity of being a pilot (i.e., weather and navigation)

Ten Months in Iran

jewelry and aftershave. In short, Frank was the quintessential asshole and I disliked him from the moment I was overpowered by his aftershave and irritated by his voice.

Priscilla was a small, mousy, subservient and pitiful woman who was about forty years old. Her clothing was neither as vogue nor as expensive as Frank's, she didn't have any jewelry on except for a small plain gold wedding band and she acted like she was too frightened to talk. I thought that my looking at her so much might be embarrassing her but then I realized that she hadn't looked up from her plate since her food arrived.

We finally got a break from Frank's mouth when he had to go take a leak. I seized the moment as quickly as possible.

"What do you teach?" I said.

"I teach physics," she said, "mostly the physics of how a helicopter can actually fly."

"Do you have a degree in physics?" I said.

"Yes, I graduated from MIT."

"Do you enjoy teaching?" I said.

"Yes, I would like to teach college somewhere when we get back home."

When her attention returned to her food, I knew that Frank must be approaching the table from behind me. Except for saying 'good bye' when we parted for the evening, she never said another word.

After Tim and I got home I asked him about Frank and Priscilla.

"What is the story behind those two?" I said.

"Isn't that union a shame?" Tim said. "She is so bright and articulate when she's not with Frank; she is a totally different person."

"Why does she put up with his shit?" I said.

42

Ten Months in Iran

"Jack," Tim said, "you don't know the half of it. He leaves her at home at night and on weekends to chase after and run around with every woman who is known to be putting out. As soon as women check in, he's after them like a fox chasing a rabbit. He must have a contact in personnel who sends him a new-woman alert."

"What does he teach?" I said.

"He teaches weather and navigation."

"What does she teach besides the physics of flight?"

"She teaches hydraulics, pneumatics, jet engine theory and she covers the mechanical stress of flight on aircraft parts."

"And she's married to, and subservient to, an asshole." I said.

"I don't think you'd get an argument from anyone about him being an asshole." Tim said.

"She looked so small, mousy and pitiful this evening, all I wanted to do was hold her in my arms and comfort her. He must be abusing her, maybe not physically but mentally." I said. "You saw how she cowers around him."

"Yes, but there's nothing you can do about it." Tim said.

An Old Friend

One evening, while having supper at the Kourosh hotel, I met Roy Wood, an old army buddy. He had been flying for Bell Helicopter for two years and would be going home in a few days. He and I were in the Second Armored Cavalry Regiment in Nuremburg, Germany when I decided to retire from the Army. He was happy to hear that I was back flying again because the last time we saw each other I was grounded, due to sinus trouble caused by the pollution in Europe, and assigned to the position of training officer for the company's Aero Rifle Platoon. I was anxious to talk to someone from my old Air Cavalry Troop because I had set up a big training

Ten Months in Iran

exercise for the Assault Platoon before leaving and wondered how it had turned out. Roy told me that my replacement was a young infantry captain assigned to the troop especially for training the assault platoon.

"I became good friends with him because I flew him to the area in Regensburg where you had planned for the operation to take place. He told me he was going to follow the training exercises and the assault plan you developed." Roy said.

"How did the Regensburg river assault go?" I said.

"Well, the first day went well. We airlifted the assault platoon to the staging area and they spent the night preparing for the river assault on the aggressor camp at dawn." Roy said.

"So," I said. "What happened on the second day?"

"The second day was a disaster. One of the troops fell out of his assault raft and drowned. It took almost ten hours to find him and pull him up from the bottom of the river." Roy said.

"Tell me it was one of the black guys." I said.

"Yes," he said. "It was a black soldier. How did you know?"

"You know the lake behind the airfield?" I said.

"Yes." He said.

"Well, I held exercises there for three days training the platoon how to escape from their combat gear in case they fell out of the raft. I placed fifteen dummy hand grenades in a back pack and had each man sit on the edge of the raft and fall into the lake backwards off the raft. We were only in four feet of water and I did it first to demonstrate how the escape was to be done. I had safety men standing on each side of the man being trained just in case someone ran into trouble releasing his gear.

After I did it I had my platoon sergeant do it and then we had all of the squad leaders do it. However, we had about eight or ten black soldiers who refused to participate in

Ten Months in Iran

the training. They sat on the bank and would not come into the water. I told them that they didn't have to know how to swim to complete this exercise and that it could save their life if they fell out of the raft during the assault. I also offered to provide a life vest to anyone who could not swim. But I told them they would still have to know how to release their combat gear, even with a vest. Not one of them came into the lake for the training; the rest of the assault platoon completed the training and then we just spent the remainder of the training time swimming and playing with the raft."

"The guy who drowned may well have been one of them because when they found him he still had all of his equipment strapped on. The only thing they didn't find was his rifle; it must still be on the bottom of the river." he said.

"That wasn't the only trouble I had with them. When we left the lake and walked back to the hanger I sent my sergeant back with a truck to pick up the raft. Someone had cut up the raft with a knife. The CO was livid because he had to explain to the Corps of Engineers major what had happened to the raft and then talk him into letting us use five additional rafts for the exercise. Our company had to pay for the destroyed raft. So, you can see, telling me that a black soldier fell out of the raft and drowned doesn't really surprise me ... or upset me either." I said.

"I can see where you wouldn't have a lot of sympathy for him." he said.

"Why did you leave the army?" I said. "You didn't have enough time in to retire."

"I was given the choice of either getting out or reverting to my enlisted rank[4]; so, I got out." he said.

---

[4] Due to the expansion of the Vietnam War, the army needed more Warrant Officers, so many qualified men were taken from the enlisted ranks of the army and sent to

Ten Months in Iran

"Did you know that if you had stayed in you would have been given back your Warrant Officer rank upon retirement?" I said.

"Yes, I knew that." he said.

"What did you do after you got out?" I said.

"I flew workers and supplies out to the oil rigs in the Gulf for a couple of years and then found this job, he said. "I thought you were going to go to work for the CIA. What happened?"

"Well, Nixon screwed the CIA with that Watergate screw up and the people I was working with, who had already told me where my assignment would be, were either let go or they bailed out. I went to Arlington after I got my separation papers and they said they had never heard of me and that they had no record of my being offered a job. The asshole I talked to said they had a new directive that they were only to hire people who had business degrees and not ex-Green Berets anymore. He said that I could fill out another employment form and that if anything came up he would call me.

About two weeks later I got a call from him over the radio telephone I was using while working for a security company in Savannah, Georgia; so, not knowing what he was going to say, I didn't know if he had found my old paperwork or was calling me on my new application. I warned him that we were talking on an open radio telephone that anyone could hear and I think it pissed him off. I never heard from him again. This was before cellular phones and everyone in the company who had one of the radio phones, including the dispatcher, could hear all conversations."

---

flight school to become helicopter pilots. After the Vietnam war was over these men (pilots) were either reduced to their previous enlisted rank or discharged.

Ten Months in Iran

"That certainly explains why the CIA is so fucked up now, doesn't it?" he said.

"Yes, if you're going to send someone into Afghanistan to aid the resistance fighters struggling against the Russians, you definitely want someone with a business degree over an ex-Green Beret." I said.

At eleven o'clock I told him that I had to get home and get some sleep or I would be worthless the next day. He had checked out of his apartment and was staying at the hotel until his flight home. I told him I would try to see him again before he left for the states.

Maggie

Maggie was one of the few female pilots in Isfahan. She was about thirty five and stood about five foot ten inches tall. Maggie was not beautiful but she was nice looking and had a terrific body. She had short brown hair and blue eyes; her best feature was her Sophia Loren lips. For as long as I knew Maggie, whenever her name came up in conversation, the first thing mentioned about her was her beautiful lips. I met her the first day I went into the pilot's locker room. She had been in Isfahan for ten months when we met. I was stowing my new flight gear in my locker when she came in dressed in a flight suit, opened a locker next to mine and sat down beside me on the long bench running between the two banks of lockers, and started to remove her boots.

"Just got here?" she said.

"Yes," I said, "this is my third day in country."

"What are you going to be doing?"

"I'm a maintenance test pilot for Cobras and a ground-school instructor." I said. "What do you do?"

"I'm and IFR[5] instructor pilot." She said.

---

[5] Instrument Flight Rules

Ten Months in Iran

At this point she threw her boots into the locker, stood up, un-zipped her flight suit and let it drop to her ankles. Then she kicked the flight suit from her feet and sat back down beside me, dressed only in her rather brief pink panties and see-thru bra. She took a small white towel from her locker and dried the perspiration from her face, arms and legs as she continued to talk.

"It's so fucking hot here; I sweat like a pig in that flight suit and by the time I get home in the evening, after the sweat has been fermenting all day, I smell like a pig. I tried to cover it up a few times with perfume but wound up smelling like a French whore."

I was dumfounded, I had no idea what to say to her. My first thought was that one of us was in the wrong locker room, but I remembered looking at the sign on the door and it said 'Pilots Lockers', not women or men, just pilots. I had to say something because the silence was killing me. I saw her name tag when she walked in so I gave it a shot.

"So, Maggie," I said, "how hot does it get here?"

"When the summer really gets going it will hit 120^0 for days at a time. You'll think you're living in hell!" she said. "Are you still at the Kourosh?"

"Yes, I haven't found a place yet."

"Oh, god, I loved staying at the Kourosh. It was so clean and cool and I didn't have to do anything. My apartment is supposed to be air conditioned but it doesn't work worth a shit. I don't think the central unit is big enough to support the load."

I placed the lock on my locker and told Maggie that I had enjoyed talking to her but I had to go over to the training facility and check in.

"I hope I get to see you again." she said.

"I think there's a good possibility in that since our lockers are side by side." I said.

Ten Months in Iran

As I left the locker room she was still sitting in her panties and bra drying her self and trying to cool off.

Isfahan Public Works

One evening, while walking home from the Kourosh hotel, I became painfully aware of the short comings of the Isfahan Public Works department. The city engineers, after digging a four foot deep hole that was about four foot square right in the middle of the sidewalk, felt they were under no obligation to block off the area so pedestrians wouldn't fall in. The only thing they felt compelled to do was to lay a small plank diagonally across the hole and place a tin can on the board. I thought for awhile maybe the tin can had been filled with oil and set on fire to create a small warning light; however, this idea proved to be wrong because none of the cans I saw were blackened by fire. I fell into the hole; lucky for me it contained only water and no sharp objects. I was also thankful that I had on jeans and a light shirt and not my good suit. After that I always carried a flashlight when walking at night.

A few weeks later on my way to work I saw an automobile with its trunk sticking up out of a deep hole in the street. Apparently the public works department didn't bother to block off holes in the street either. However, I did see the obligatory plank and tin can on the street near the car. During my eleven months in Iran I saw a number of cars, trucks and motorcycles stuck in holes in sidewalks and streets. Holes in the street were not the only hazard one had to contend with in Iran. On several occasions I turned a corner, either walking or driving, and encountered large pieces of potentially dangerous equipment operating with no warning signs or barriers to restrict or redirect traffic. I guess I'll never know why the

Ten Months in Iran

concept of blocking off an obstruction or a hazardous area never caught on in Iran.

I was particularly frustrated by this endemic lack of concern for safety because one of my duties at the airbase was to teach safety rules and procedures to be followed when working around aircraft and other large pieces of equipment used to service aircraft. After conducting several safety classes with little to no perceptible interest, I came up with a unique method to make them pay attention.

I learned early on that Iranians evidently had no thought of preventing their accidental death because they believed that the date of their death was already written down. So, whenever possible, I told them that they probably wouldn't be killed if they did something in a particular way but that they would probably just be maimed for life. They weren't afraid of dying but they were afraid of going through life without a hand, arm or leg; I concentrated on getting pictures of people who had been mangled but not killed to use in my safety classes. The resulting level of interest demonstrated by the class and the general change in attitude was remarkable. I also benefited because my class's grades went up and that made me look good as an instructor.

Another encounter with Maggie

After using the pilot's locker room for some time and not running into anyone else, except Maggie on the first day, I asked one of the pilots on the flight line about it.

"Many of the pilots," he said, "don't use the locker room; they wear their flight suits all day so they just come to work in them. The pilots who do use the locker room put their suits on in the morning and spend the day with their students and don't take them off until they go home in the

Ten Months in Iran

evening; so, unless you were there early in the morning or late in the afternoon, you would never see them."
"The only person I have ever seen in there is Maggie." I said.
"That's because she has a special job of teaching and testing mostly senior Iranian pilots to fly IFR. She's really something, isn't she?" he said.
"Something is right!" I said. "She came in and stripped down to her panties and bra right in front of me."
"Oh, that's nothing." he said. "Wait until you run into her in the shower. That's why the Iranian instructor pilots and students were banned from using our locker room; they would hang around waiting for her to show up and then crowd into the locker room. We couldn't get anything done while she was in the area."
"I can't wait." I said.

That bit of information made me wonder about Maggie's psychological condition. What would make a nice looking intelligent woman do the things that she did. She acted like some ugly woman who felt compelled to jump on any man who showed the least bit of interest in her because, in her mind, he may be her last chance. I thought she must have had some type of psychological brain damage caused by something that happened to her when she was young, something her father said, something her mother said or maybe something that she just overheard when she was young. Something has released an uncontrollable exhibitionist desire in her.

Setting a date with Maggie

Maggie came in and sad down beside me while I was having lunch at the airfield.
"I haven't seen you in weeks. What have you been doing?" she said.

Ten Months in Iran

"I've been busy teaching and test flying Cobras." I said. "What have you been up to?"

"I'm still trying to teach old farts to fly IFR."

"Why older pilots?" I said.

"Because they never had to fly IFR when they went through flight training due to the fact that the helicopters they were flying weren't IFR rated. The helicopters they have today, except for your Cobra, are all IFR rated and the flight students learn to fly IFR in school; and the older pilots will not go to school with the young students." she said.

"I hate flying IFR." I said. "It takes all the fun out of flying."

"Well, these old boys don't like it either. I think that's why they hired me."

"I can see where having you as an instructor would make the process a lot more enjoyable." I said.

"Are you still at the Kourosh?" she said.

"No, I rented a house over by the university. I'm sharing it with a friend who also works for Bell. He's a language instructor."

"That's a good area to be in. Is it a new house?"

"I think it's about three or four years old." I said. "Is your air conditioner working yet?"

"Not really. But, I did buy several fans and they make my apartment a lot more tolerable to live in." She said.

"Where do you live?" I said.

"Compared with where you live; I live in the slums." she said.

"Why didn't you join with someone and share the rent so you could get a better place?"

"I can't do that. If I lived with a man he would think that he owned me and that would be the end of that. If I lived with a woman we would probably kill each other over boyfriends." she said.

52

Ten Months in Iran

At that point I was looking for a way out so I looked at my watch and told her that I had to go test fly an aircraft.

About a week later I was working outside the hangar that housed the pilot's locker room. I had just completed motoring[6] both engines of a Cobra on the flight line so the ground maintenance crew could wash the engines out with solvent. We waited thirty minutes and then I started the right engine and they were supposed to use water to complete the task. However, the airman picked up the solvent sprayer instead of the water sprayer and shot it into the intake of the running jet engine. A severe compressor stall occurred that sounded like a mortar round had landed beside the aircraft. The airman fell off the wing and on his way to the ground sprayed me with solvent. I called the maintenance desk on the radio and told them about the problem, entered it into the aircraft's log book and went to the locker room for a shower and a clean flight suit.

The shower room was an eight by twelve foot room with shower heads located around the walls at an interval of about five feet. I was washing my hair when I heard one of the other showers come on; I rinsed the soap from my face and looked across the room to see Maggie washing her hair. Here breasts looked much better without her bra smashing them down. I watched, and envied, the soap as it ran over and around her large breasts, across her flat stomach to her pubic hair and finally down her shapely legs to the floor. I was getting an erection as she rinsed the soap from her eyes and looked at me. I immediately turned around and hit the cold water valve.
"Well," she said, "you're not dead after all."
"What do you mean, I'm not dead?" I said.

---

[6] turning the engine without starting it

Ten Months in Iran

"I can see that you've finally noticed me." she said. "I've been dropping hints ever since we met that I would like to go home with you but you never acted like you were interested. I began to think you had a problem; however, I can see that you don't."

The cold water was not doing its job so I grabbed my towel and left the shower room. After a sufficient amount of blood returned to my brain, I stuck my head into the shower room and asked her if she would like to meet me at the Kourosh for supper that evening at seven o'clock. She said she would be there.

I headed back over to the aircraft so I could talk to the quality control inspector who would be checking the engine for possible damage from the compressor stall. The inspector was a young ex-airforce sergeant named Tom Mix who had graduated from GE[7]'s in-factory jet engine maintenance training, so he really knew what he was doing. I told him what had happened and that after the compressor stall, all engine parameters returned to normal. His name intrigued me so I had to ask.

"Were you named after a movie star cowboy?" I said.

"Yes, I was." he said. "Were you a Tom Mix fan too?"

"Actually, I was a Tex Ritter fan."

"Dad told me about him too." he said.

"I guess you never had to explain or defend your name in school since the kids you went to school with probably never heard of Tom Mix the cowboy." I said.

"Back in the fifties TV would occasionally show old Tom Mix movies so I ran into a few kids who had seen him on TV." he said. "But, they thought it was neat to have a cowboy name."

"I used to go to the movies every Saturday and see Tex Ritter, Tom Mix, Roy Rogers and Gene Autry." I said. "I

---

[7] General Electric

Ten Months in Iran

think I got my moral values from those cowboys and not from church as my mother always thought. Those cowboy movies taught me to always be honest and tell the truth, always treat a woman like a lady, always protect the weak, always stand up to evil and never hit someone who is down."

"You sound just like my dad." he said. "He thinks the only thing movies teach kids today is to react with violence when faced with any unexpected situation."

"Well, I think I would have to agree with him." I said. "You hear so many stories today about bullies in the schools; I only ran into two bullies in all of my school days and I beat the crap out of both of them. I knew a third boy who was not a bully but liked to fight; so, he would act like he had a speech impediment and when someone laughed at him he would beat up on them. He tried it with me only I didn't laugh at him; I just tried my best to understand what he was saying. We became good friends after that. I never did find out what his problem was but he didn't like it when anyone laughed at anyone else because of some physical or mental disability. I saw him beat the crap out of a boy once because he was making fun of a little kid who had hydrocephalus."

"Where are you from, sir?" he asked.

"Ohio," I said, "why?"

"I just wondered," he said, "my dad is from Indiana. You have the same ideas; I thought you may have come from the same place."

"Could be," I said, "they're both Midwestern states."

We watched as the Iranian ground crew set up the checkstands around the aircraft and opened the inspection doors. Tom picked up his tool box and placed it on the stand.

"I'd better get to work here or I'll never get this job completed." he said.

Ten Months in Iran
An evening with Maggie

I arrived at the Kourosh hotel fifteen minutes early and waited in the lobby for Maggie to arrive. As each taxi arrived, I stood up and walked to the door. Seven o'clock arrived and passed and no Maggie. I began to think that she was not going to show up. At seven fifteen she stepped out of her taxi and, as she stood by the driver's window paying her fare, all activity at the entrance of the hotel stopped because every man was frozen in place looking at Maggie. She had on a red silk dress that was too tight, too low and too short. It was apparent, even to the most casual observer, that she couldn't possibly have anything else on under her dress because she had no panty lines, no bra lines and her long tan legs were bare. I wondered, as she walked into the lobby, how she could possibly sit down without exposing herself. She kissed me on the cheek and told me she was sorry that she was late. The lobby had been quite noisy before she arrived; there were twenty to thirty people all talking loud and in different languages. As we walked to the elevator, the lobby was so quiet I could hear the soft tap of her high heals on the floor. We were alone in the elevator to the club restaurant.

"Do I look ok?" she said.

"I don't think ok is quite the word for it. I was thinking more along the line of devastating. Where did you get that dress? I know you didn't get it here."

"I got it in Paris." she said.

"If I were you," I said, "I'd be careful where I wore it because I think you could be arrested for wearing that dress here. You could give one of these old Iranian farts a heart attack, you know some of them have never even seen a woman's ankle, and be charged with his murder."

"This is the first time I've ever had it on." She said.

"I think I would restrict it to private parties." I said.

Ten Months in Iran

I selected a table near the back of the room where we wouldn't be too conspicuous. We managed to have a nice quiet supper together without causing any alarms to go off. I thought we would be safe as long as she didn't get up, and she didn't. Lucky for me she didn't want to dance. We had another lucky break when leaving, the lobby was empty.

As I helped her into my jeep, my suspicion that she couldn't sit down without exposing her self was confirmed.

I understood as soon as I saw Maggie's apartment why she said she couldn't live with anyone and the explanation she had given to me was not the reason. Maggie was a slob. She apologized before we even stepped inside that she hadn't cleaned her apartment in a few days. After going inside, I would say that she hadn't cleaned her apartment in a few months. There were dirty clothes, dirty dishes, used paper plates and cups, beer cans and soda cans everywhere. Her couch looked like some wild animal had been using it for a nest. She said she was going to fix us a drink and walked into the kitchen. I followed her to make sure that what ever she intended to put my drink in was washed first. The kitchen was even a bigger disaster than the living room. I had seen abandoned buildings that were in better shape. As I stood there watching her wash a glass for my drink I noticed handwriting on the refrigerator; I walked over for a closer look and discovered that her fridge had a list of about 25 or 30 men's names written on it; they were all signatures of men. The very first name on the list was none other than my favorite asshole Frank Swick, Priscilla's husband.

"Why all the signatures on you refrigerator?" I said.

"Oh," she said, "I don't know how that got started; but, those are names of men who have been my guests."

"I see you've met Frank?" I said.

"Oh, do you mean Needle Dick Swick?"

Ten Months in Iran

"Needle dick?" I said.

"Yes, not only does he have a tiny dick, he doesn't know what to do with it. I'm sure you've heard the saying 'slam bam thank you mam'. Well, he doesn't even get through the slam before he pops off; with Frank, there is no 'bam' to talk about."

Talk about getting more information than you really wanted. I could have survived nicely without hearing that story. Well, honey, I thought, my name isn't going on your refrigerator. Now, I thought, how am I going to get out of this without pissing her off? I had no intention of being her next trophy but I also didn't want to become her enemy. I didn't want to sit on the couch because I wasn't sure what had been sleeping there; so I sat down on an overstuffed chair.

As I drank my drink, she went into the bedroom and changed out of her dress and into a nightgown that was even more revealing; when she came back into the room she sat down on my lap. The stress of the situation was giving me a severe headache. I also had one of those painful erections where so much blood is pumped into your penis that it causes small skin lacerations just behind the head. I wanted to have sex with her so badly, and probably would have added my name to her trophy list, but I was not going to join any group that had Frank Swick as a charter member.

"I think we have a problem here." I said.

"What problem?" she said. "I can feel you dick trying to work its way into my ass now!"

"You have rules that you live by, like never dating the same man twice and never sharing an apartment with a man. I also have some rules that I've always lived by and one of them is to never jump a woman on the first date. I've found that the whole experience is better if you wait

Ten Months in Iran

until the second or even third date when you know each other better." I said.

"You've got to be kidding me!" she said.

"No, it's true. I don't do it on the first date; and since you don't ever allow a second date, we have a problem. I'd really like to make love to you, but not tonight."

I could feel her body relax as she leaned back and thought about what I said. She was quiet for a long time and then asked me a question.

"Can we just fool around without fucking? You do like to kiss and just play with a girl's body, don't you?" she said.

"Yes," I said. "I'd like to play with you."

I spent the remainder of the evening kissing and fondling her; I did everything except have sexual intercourse with her; she did manage a final, and welcomed, *coup de grace* by performing oral sex on me. I got out without signing her refrigerator.

Foreign Workers

Isfahan had a large number of foreign workers employed in a great number of disciplines. There were Filipino nurses and doctors, Korean and Filipino waiters and cooks (Iranians, Afghans, Indians and Bangladeshis wouldn't handle bacon). There were oil field engineers from the United Stated, Britain, Russia and France; teachers from the United States, Britain and France and airline pilots from the United States and Britain. You could meet all of these people at one time or another at the Kourosh hotel.

I became friends with an American flight line maintenance worker named Jay who introduced me to five Filipino nurses who lived together in an apartment in Isfahan. Jay was from New York and a slick operator. He always had something going and I'm not sure that it was always legal. He always had too much money for what I

Ten Months in Iran

knew his pay grade earned and he had a big apartment all to himself.

He was giving a party for all of his friends and as it turned out, he had a lot of them. I met and became acquainted with more people during his party than I had at any other time.

When he invited me he told me that the five nurses would be there. I was very interested because I hadn't met anyone I was interested in yet; however, once at the party it became apparent that Mai, the only pretty nurse there, was Jay's girlfriend. Mai was not your typical Filipino girl. I always thought she was probably the product of an American sailor stationed in the Philippines and a Filipino mother. Mai was taller than the other girls, her skin was several shades lighter and her short black hair was curly. She was also a little older than the other nurses and clearly the group's leader. The other nurses weren't ugly but they were too skinny, extremely plain and lacked any personality traits that would have carried them past their looks.

A few days later, as a favor to Mai, I agreed to transport Amelda, one of the nurses, across town so that she could complete some task that she had. But the trip was aborted less than three blocks from her apartment.

The trouble started when I arrived at her apartment fifteen minutes early. She bitched at me for being too early and that she wasn't ready. Then she bitched at me for having my flight suit on and that it would attract attention to us as we drove through town; then she bitched at me because I had an open jeep and that the top was down. Her final bitch was that she didn't like the route that I was taking to the address she had given to me. At that point that I returned to her building, told her to "get out of the car" and I went back to work at the airfield.

Ten Months in Iran

I saw Jay the next day and told him what had happened and he just laughed and told me that he was well aware of Amelda's lack of social graces. I continued to see Jay and Mai but I stayed away from the nurses' apartment.

Unexpected meeting with Priscilla

I saw Priscilla walking between the training buildings and ran over to her.
"Priscilla, how're you doing?"
"Jack," she said, "what're you doing here?"
"I work in the other building. I teach exactly the same subjects that you do, except most of my students are enlisted men."
"Where are you going?" she said.
"Well, I don't know. Where are you going?" I said.
"I'm going to get something to eat."
"Good, I'll get something too, if you don't mind?"
"I'd love to have you join me." she said.
Tim was right, Priscilla was bright and articulate when out from under her husband's thumb. We talked for almost half and hour about our work and about Iran. I asked her where Frank was and she told me that he had a lot of vacation time built up and was afraid that he was going to lose it so he went to Greece for a week. I didn't have the heart to ask her why she hadn't gone with him. I told her that I would like to have lunch with her again some time and she told me that she was there every day at about the same time.

The Medical Practice

Jay invited me to another party at his apartment and assured me that Amelda would not be there; so, I accepted. I was surprised to see Tom Mix at the party; I didn't know he and Jay knew each other.

Ten Months in Iran

"Tom," I said, "we meet again." I said.

"Jack, how are you doing?" he said.

"I didn't know you and Jay were friends."

"The American community here is relatively small and sooner of later you meet everyone if you're a party person." He said.

"I guess I'm not that much of a party person." I said. "I only know about ten Americans in Isfahan."

"Keep coming to Jay's parties and you'll meet just about everyone. He introduced me to my girlfriend, Farah. I'll always be in debt to him for that."

"Is she here?" I said.

"No, not tonight; she's with her aunt." he said.

We talked about the problems we ran into living in Iran and some of the solutions we had discovered. Tom talked about sending most of his money to a bank in the states and only keeping enough on hand to cover expenses. He wanted to go back to the states after his contract was up and go to college.

During the party Mai complained about Iranian men and told us about conditions at the hospital. She worked in the maternity ward and told us stories that were unbelievable. She said that a doctor could not look directly at a woman's vagina; the doctor (male or female) had to use a mirror during a physical exam. Babies were born under a sheet and if the mother needed stitches, the doctor did the job by looking at his subject with a mirror.

Mai told us that pregnant women were treated like they had a disease and that most men didn't like to touch them. The older men, she said, didn't even come to the hospital when their wives were giving birth and that other women in the family would pick them up and take them home. Women who had girl babies first were treated very poorly and sometimes even abused by their husbands for giving them a girl as their first born. One woman told Mai that

Ten Months in Iran

her little girl was two years old before her husband ever saw her and even then he ignored her.

Mai said that Amelda worked in the emergency room and told her that only about one in one hundred children seen in the emergency room is a girl. If a boy gets a serious injury he is taken to the emergency room. If a girl gets a serious injury she is treated at home and only taken to the emergency room if her mother thinks she is in danger of dying.

Ten Months in Iran

Chapter 2
Christina

Bob, a good friend of mine who was an aircraft mechanic for Bell, was in a traffic accident and was forced to support the victim's family because he claimed that he couldn't work due to the accident. Bob told me that the man jumped out in front of him just as he was stopping at a traffic sign and that he hardly made contact with him. However, the man conveniently had witnesses standing by when the police arrived. Bob had his family with him and was in debt the whole time he was in Iran due to the staged accident. His sixteen year old daughter Christina suffered a little more than her younger brother because she was going to an American school and had no money for new clothes or the other things that young girls need money for at school.

Christina was a beautiful, well developed young girl with shoulder length red hair and green eyes. She was about five foot six inches tall and a few pounds overweight. She asked me one day if I would give her a job cleaning my house so she could earn some money. I didn't really need anyone to clean my house but this was a way to help her out without making it look like charity. I made arrangements with her mother to pick her up every Saturday morning so she could help me clean. You didn't

Ten Months in Iran

have to be around her long to realize that although she was a beautiful young girl and well on her way to being a woman, she was more than a little crude. She was a daddy's girl and daddy hadn't taught her much in the way of social manners or etiquette. But you can't expect someone to teach something of which they have little knowledge. Bob liked the macho sports; wrestling, prize fighting, drag racing and stock car racing and he liked his sports with a cold beer. He was a loveable, good natured, good-old-boy from Alabama who was under-educated and unsophisticated, man who had learned his trade in the Air Force and was a very good aircraft mechanic. Unfortunately for his daughter, his wife Alice wasn't a tower of social graces either.

She was also raised on a farm in Alabama and taught that her top three priorities in life were her husband, her children and her house; and, as much as I was able to observe, she didn't show much interest in anything outside of those three areas of responsibility. Alice was a stout farm girl, a terrific cook, a good housekeeper and just as lovable as her husband. She had a sort of plain, clean and scrubbed Southern beauty about her, she was very pleasant to be around and you couldn't ask for a better friend.

Since Christina was Bob's only child for about eight years until his son finally arrived, she served as, and was treated like, the son he wanted to pal around with. Her little brother was just now getting old enough that her dad could do father-son things with him; so, the time she would normally spend with her dad was being infringed upon and I think she was feeling the loss of his attention. I think that was the reason she latched onto me almost as soon as we were introduced. I also think she expected, or at least hoped, to have the same type of relationship with me that she had with her father and that never happened; I always treated her like a lady and expected her to act like

65

a lady. The journey from tomboy to lady was not short or easy; there were things that she needed to hear and learn that I couldn't say or teach.

Those Remarkable Isfahan Cats

Christina and her family lived in a built up area of multistory apartments. They were on the second floor and had a beautiful balcony overlooking the street and the courtyards on the other side of the street. They had no TV so, when I visited, we spent a lot of time on the balcony watching the world go by. The most entertaining thing to watch were the acrobatic stunts performed by the many cats that lived in the neighborhood. There were almost no trees, only mud or concrete walls and houses. That did not deter the cats of Isfahan. They had, over the years, adjusted superbly to their environment.

I never saw a fat cat in Isfahan; they were large thin cats and I think they lived by killing and eating rats that were nearly as big as they were. I saw Isfahan cats repeatedly jump a horizontal distance of ten to twelve feet with apparent ease. They would jump from a wall to the top of a car parked in a courtyard and then from that car to the next wall. As many hours as I watched the cats from my friend's balcony I never saw a cat on the ground, they were always on the walls, cars or roof tops.

One day as I watched a cat walking along the top of the wall parallel to the street, he made a turn onto the wall dividing the courtyards and started towards the house; about four feet from the house the cat jumped up six to eight feet into the air and went through a drain hole in the wall and onto the roof. I also saw cats climb to the roofs of buildings by going up the wall like it was a tree.

Ten Months in Iran
Tea and Sympathy

I was having lunch and Priscilla came in and sat down across the table from me.

"Do you mind if I join you?" she said.

"It'll be the best think that's happened to me today." I said.

"Having a tough day?" she said.

"No, actually I've had a good morning. But, nothing that's happened so far can compare with the pleasure of your company."

"Thank you, Jack. I enjoy your company too. I was hoping you'd be here; I've been trying to run into you for two days. I need to talk to someone and you're the only person I've met since I've been here that I feel comfortable with. I know some of the other wives but if you tell them something you might as well print it in the company new letter."

"What do you want to talk about? Do you need help?" I said.

"No, I don't want any help. I just need to talk and I need someone to listen."

"Well, I'm good at that. I have five daughters and I do a lot of listening and no one pays any attention to my advice anyway."

"You have five daughters?" she said.

"Yes, I do, and they're all beautiful intelligent ladies now. Their names are: Mary Linda, Viola Suzanne, Bianca Marie, Frances Monique and Heidi Georgia Ann."

"You're so lucky." she said. "I want children but Frank doesn't want any; and by the way our marriage is going maybe it's a good thing we don't have children. He's so controlling, he won't allow me to do anything or go anywhere outside of work. He goes away alone and he goes out at night alone, but I have to stay in the apartment. I think he's going out with other women. No, who am I

Ten Months in Iran

trying to kid? I know he's going out with other women. Frank is a sex nut; we were married just before we came over here and, for the first year, he had to have sex three or four times a week.

Then, over a period of about three months, we went from sex three or four times a week to three or four times a month; and for the past three months we haven't had sex at all. We aren't having sex at all and I catch him in the bathroom masturbating. Do you see something wrong with this picture? I thought for awhile that he may have caught something and just didn't want to give it to me. But nothing he could catch over here would last more than two or three penicillin shots."

She was quiet for awhile as she drank her tea. I didn't say a word. I just waited for her to continue because I could tell she had a lot more on her mind.

"He doesn't allow me to talk to anyone. He would be furious if he knew I was talking to you - and if he knew what we were talking about, he would be livid. He was such a gentleman when we first started dating; he was so tall, good looking and intelligent. How was I to know that he would turn into a possessive tyrant?"

She stopped again, drank more of her tea and picked at her food. I felt so sorry for her. I wanted to tell her to drop that asshole and take your life back but I didn't. I had to keep telling myself 'Jack, keep your mouth shut'.

"You know, Jack," she said, "women who are in love do some really stupid things. He talked me into having my pay check deposited with his pay check in the bank; the only trouble is he has the only check book and the bank won't talk to me. So, even if I wanted to run away, I can't because I have no money. He gives me a small allowance, 'just enough to keep me out of trouble' he says. My mother told me I was thinking with my ass when I told her we were going to get married. I should've listened to her."

Ten Months in Iran

I could tell by the inflection in her voice during her last comment that she was finished. So, I decided to talk.

"Do you feel better now?" I said.

"No, I don't, but, I do feel a little relieved. Thanks for listening to me rant and rave."

"Any time you feel like ranting and raving, just look me up and I'll listen to you."

I looked back at her as I left the room; she was still sitting there picking at her food.

It was only about a week later that I saw Priscilla looking through the window in the door to my classroom. She motioned for me to come to her. She was under a great deal of stress; her eyes and nose were red from crying and she was shaking. She handed me a small piece of paper that was wadded up and wet from her tears; it was a note from Frank.

> *Priscilla,*
> *I'm taking a 5am flight to the states. I'll send you an address where you can send the divorce papers.*
> *Frank*

My first thought was that she was lucky to be rid of him, but, I knew she wouldn't see it that way right now. So I offered her my support and sympathy.

"That son-of-bitch took off with all our money; he has the check book and today is the day he normally gives me my allowance. I can't believe he did this to me! What the hell have I ever done to him, except try to be a good wife and do whatever he told me to do?"

"The first thing we have to do is get you calmed down so you can go to the personnel office and let them know what has happened. You need to have them stop your

69

check from being deposited in his account and, if possible, retract the last deposit."
"Can they do that?" she said.
"Yes, they can, if we talk to the right person." I said.
We stopped and had a cup of tea to get her settled down enough to talk to personnel. I gave her two hundred dollars to live on until she got some money from Bell. And just having some money in her hand seemed to have a calming affect on her. I told her if that ran out I would give her some more. She was lucky and got a senior female personnel manager to talk to her. I sat in the waiting room for thirty minutes while they talked in the manager's office. When she came out, she looked like a different woman.
"From the look on your face, I'd say she is going to help you." I said.
"Yes, she is. She must have made five telephone calls to the states while I was in there. She had his pay frozen. So his paycheck won't be deposited either." she said.
"I said it could be done if you got the right person, and you did."
She had a totally different attitude about the situation on the way back over to the training buildings. She thanked me and went back to work.

Priscilla's Transformation

It didn't take Priscilla long to adjust to her newly found freedom. I saw her in the lunch room a week later sitting with a group of people, and she was talking and laughing. I was so happy to see that she was finally able to make friends of her own. I didn't join them. I sat as far away as I could and enjoyed watching her enjoy herself.

The next day, I saw Priscilla's face in my classroom door again. And again she motioned for me to come to her.

Ten Months in Iran

When I stepped into the hallway she handed me two hundred dollars and thanked me for lending it to her, then she invited me to have supper with her at the Kourosh hotel that evening. I accepted.

I arrived early to be there when she arrived; but, to my surprise, she was already there.
"You must have gotten her early." I said.
"Actually," she said, "I'm staying here until I go home Monday."
"Your going home Monday?"
"Yes, I've got to get back to take care of my problem with Frank. I don't want to leave. I'm just now starting to enjoy myself."
"This is certainly a disappointment to me." I said. "I was hoping to get to know you better. I was also just starting to enjoy myself."
"Well, thank you, Jack. I didn't know you were interested in me."
"Priscilla, the only reason I can think of for a man not to be interested in you is if he's queer."
She laughed at my remark as we took the elevator to the club restaurant. All traces of the small, mousy, subservient and pitiful little woman who I had met that first night were gone. Her transformation was nothing short of miraculous; I was more attracted to her now than before.
"Are you coming back?" I said.
"No, I tried to get them to take me back after I get my problem worked out but they wouldn't even talk about it."
"I wish we'd had more time together. It will be lonely around here just knowing that I won't run into you during lunch." I said.
We had a rather quiet supper together. I did manage to dance with her a few times; My enjoyment of holding her in my arms for the first time was tainted by the knowledge

71

Ten Months in Iran

that it would also be the last time. On the elevator, I asked her what floor she was on and pushed that button. She intercepted my hand and stopped me from pushing the ground floor button.

"Come with me." she said.

The tone of her voice and the touch of her hand caused an avalanche of sexual desire to be released within my body. By the time we got inside her room I had an erection that was beyond concealment. She threw her purse onto the dresser and pressed against me.

"Oh!" she said as she pushed away and looked down at the bulge in my paints. "Oh, my goodness, you do like me, don't you?"

I didn't say anything; I just picked her up, placed her on the bed and eased myself down beside her. We kissed for several minutes before I removed her blouse and bra. We kissed a few more minutes. I moved down to suck on her small but very firm breasts, then her belly button. As I kissed her stomach, I unzipped her skirt and pulled it down exposing a small pair of red panties. I kissed all around the edges of her panties and then placed my mouth over her pubic area and softly exhaled my hot breath; she wiggled, moaned and tilted her pelvis up to my mouth. I pulled her red panties down and she kicked her skirt and panties to the floor. I stood up, removed my clothes and positioned myself between her legs. She flinched a few times as I entered her.

"Are you ok?" I said.

"You're so big." she said.

"Honey, from the articles I've read, I'm about average."

"If you're average, my husband is a midget. You're twice, no, three times as big."

"You haven't been with many men, have you?" I said.

"Just my husband and now, you." she said.

I thought about Maggie and her nickname for Frank and was not surprised that Priscilla thought I was big. I was

Ten Months in Iran

thankful then for the relief that Maggie had given me because it allowed me to last longer since I hadn't had any other sex in months.

"Wrap your arms and legs around me." I said.

"What are you going to do?" she said.

"I'll show you."

Priscilla place her arms and legs around me, I picked her up and sat on the side of the bed with her on my lap.

"Well, that's different. I've never done that before." she said.

I held her and kissed her as she bounced her up and down on me.

"This is fun; I like this."

After awhile I pulled her knees up, pushed back and had her sit on top of me.

"Oh, this is fun too."

This position gave her too much control and I couldn't get her to slow down; after a few minutes I had a climax. I could see a disappointed look come over her face when she realized what had happened.

"It's not over yet." I said. "All we have to do is rest for a few minutes and I'll be ready to go again."

She went to the bathroom and returned with a warm wash cloth. She sat down beside me; my penis was still erect, and wrapped it like a baby in the warm cloth and kissed it on the head.

"There now," she said, "you rest for awhile; I have more work for you."

We made love twice that night and again in the morning before going to breakfast. I spent the weekend with her at the hotel and she left for the states that Monday while I was at work. I was depressed for a week after she left. I didn't want to go anywhere and I didn't want to do anything.

73

Ten Months in Iran
A Rainy Day in Isfahan

My house wasn't far from the downtown section of Isfahan so I frequently walked when I had business in town or just wanted to go out and get something to eat at my favorite Korean restaurant or the Kourosh hotel. It was during such a day that I had my first experience with an Isfahan rainy day. I had been in Isfahan for a few months and had witnessed only brief showers that were gone quickly and the residue evaporated within minutes. This rain was different; it didn't stop for almost three hours. The Zayandeh River runs through the South end of Isfahan and its level is usually several feet below the level of the city so you would think it would be easy to drain the city of any heavy rain that fell.

The people who built the ancient city of Aspadana (now Isfahan) and Shah Abbas the Great who reorganized and rebuilt Isfahan around 1590 gave no thought to rain except to let nature take its course; and nature's course was to collect the rain in three to four foot deep lakes within the city. After the rain stopped I tried to walk home but found most of my normal routes blocked by water that was too high to walk through. I did walk for several blocks through water that was up to my knees at times and was in constant fear that I would fall into one of the unmarked holes that public works had left in the sidewalk. Every time I saw a tin can or a plank float passed I was struck by fear.

Some of the water was finding its way out of the city and into the river but it was not by any planned route. The whole city came to a halt until most of the water had soaked into the sandy soil or found some other escape route. Several cars were flooded and stalled in the streets. The city buses were running and causing two-foot-high wakes in the standing water, wakes that were causing

Ten Months in Iran

further havoc in the street-side stores that were already flooded. You could see the shop owners shaking their fists at the bus drivers every time one passed.

I was concerned about my house but found out that my neighborhood was built on top of a small hill and that we didn't have to worry about flooding. I was amazed that a city that had been there for a thousand years hadn't constructed some type of drain system to take the excess rain water to the river.

Sohila

I met Sohila at Jay's apartment one Saturday afternoon a few weeks after Priscilla had returned to the states. I didn't really feel like going to a party but Jay talked me into it. I think it was his attempt to get me out of my emotional slump. She was sitting in a corner with her back to me talking to her older sister Soraya. I first saw her face when I was introduced to others in the room and she looked over her shoulder at me. She was wearing a chador with no veil and the black cloth formed a contrasting oval frame around her beautiful white face. She pulled the cover from her head as she looked at me and exposed her shoulder length black hair. She had dark eyes and full red lips. I couldn't take my eyes off her as I wondered what the rest of her looked like. I found out that she and her sister had been shopping and she had worn the chador to the gold bazaar to keep from having any trouble.

It wasn't long before she stood up and took it off. She was about five foot two inches tall, slightly overweight, big breasted and a very beautiful young woman. It took me about five minutes to work my way around the room and put myself in position where I could talk to her. I introduced myself and told her that I had only been in Iran for a few weeks and that I was a pilot for Bell Helicopter.

Ten Months in Iran

Soraya asked me where I was from in the states and I told her I was originally from Ohio, but I had left Ohio when I was seventeen to join the Navy. She then asked me, in a rather snippy voice, how much education I had if I left school when I was seventeen. I told her that I actually dropped out of high school to join the Navy but by the time I got out of the service I had completed seven years of college with a major in physics. That bit of information apparently changed her attitude and she became very friendly.

Sohila seemed attracted to me right away and I let her know that I was attracted to her. I spent the rest of my time at the party talking to her and her sister. Before the party ended Soraya asked me if I would like to go to her house for the evening meal. I accepted her invitation and asked her to write her address down so I could take a taxi to her house. She told me that I could just go home with them after the party and that she would take me home later that night. I was a little taken back by Soraya's boldness; it was something I wasn't expecting from a woman in a Muslim country. During our conversation I found out that Sohila was a Sunni Muslim, twenty five years old (fourteen years younger than I) and a graduate of Isfahan University where she majored in languages. She spoke perfect English and, I was told later by Tim, that she also spoke excellent French and Italian.

Her father had been a professor at the university but was retired and ever since her mother died she had been dedicated to taking care of him. She lived with him most of the time and only occasionally stayed with her sister.
Soraya was a very big lady, about six feet tall and must have weighed around 190 pounds. She was about twenty pounds overweight but was still an extremely lovely lady. I guessed her age to be about fifty-five. She dressed in the

Ten Months in Iran

latest Western styles and demonstrated an impeccable taste in clothing. I knew she was a widow but I never found out what happened to her husband. She never offered an explanation and I never asked. She had two sons who were seventeen and nineteen; Reza, the seventeen year old lived at home and the older boy was out making a living on his own. Soraya's home was my first exposure to an Iranian's home and her house proved to be representative of what I had read about typical Iranian homes. I followed her lead and removed my shoes when we entered the house. We walked through a short hallway and into a twelve by twelve room that had nothing in it except a beautiful thick rug on the floor and several cushions around the wall. She asked me to sit down while she prepared some food. One side of the room had four glass sliding doors that opened onto a courtyard located in the center of the house. I could see that all four sides of the courtyard were glass and I watched Soraya as she walked around to the kitchen located on the opposite side. It was an open air courtyard but not a place where you could take a walk. It was twelve foot square with one bench and a tree in the middle that were surrounded by flowers and bushes.

Sohila opened the door to a storage area built into the wall and pulled out a small tape player and placed it on the floor.
"What type of music do you like? she said.
"I like all types of music."
"Well, then I'll play something that I like."
I found myself listening to Frank Sinatra crooning *New York, New York*. After listening to three or four more songs by Sinatra, she opened the storage area again and took out a large lace-trimmed white cloth and placed it in the center of the rug. Another trip to the storage area produced some dishes, glasses and silverware. When

Ten Months in Iran

Soraya started delivering the food the 'table' was set and ready. Sohila excused herself and left the room for a short period and, I thought, went to wash her hands. When she came back I asked to wash my hands. Our supper was a typical Iranian evening meal - a salad of chicken, peas, potatoes and mayonnaise. The salad was followed by a kebab of lamb, tomatoes, onions and lemon. We also had bread, cheese and honey followed by baklava. She ended the meal with saffron and nut flavored ice cream served with coffee. I had never eaten a regular meal while sitting on the floor and I soon found out that it was not as easy as one might think.

I had trouble coordinating the process of holding my plate, using the silverware, using the salt and pepper, parking my coffee and what to do with my bread? I noticed that neither Soraya nor Sohila picked up their plate but trying to lean over my plate the way they were was killing my back. The ladies were either unaware of my plight or just ignoring my clumsy attempt to eat without getting my feet on the 'table cloth' or spilling my drink while trying to set it down on the soft thick rug. I finally made it through the meal without, I think, creating any major social blunders. But I did apologize for my clumsiness and I did remember to pass everything with my right hand.

After the meal was over we sat and talked about what they wanted to talk about, where I was from in the United States, California and my family.

"I'm from a little town called Newark, in the state of Ohio. It's about thirty miles East of Columbus, the capital city." I said.

"That's where Ohio State University is." Sohila said. "My father picked that school as one of his choices for me to take my graduate training in English."

"Did you go?" I said.

Ten Months in Iran

"No, I went to the Sorbonne in Paris because they offered my father a better deal."

"Did you enjoy yourself in Paris?" I said.

"Soraya and I had a great time in Paris, although I think she had a greater time than I did because while I was in class, she was free to do what ever she wanted to do."

I looked at Soraya; she raised her eyebrows, looked up in the air, shook her head back and forth with a little smile and gave me that 'I'll-never-tell' look. Sohila's comment and Soraya's bold attitude with me earlier in the day told me that she was a frisky one.

"Did you go to Ohio State?" Soraya said.

"As a matter of fact," I said, "I was attending Ohio State when I got my job with Bell Helicopter. I had to drop out to take the job."

"What were you studying?" Sohila said.

"I was working on an advanced degree in English."

"But, you said your major was in physics." Sohila said.

"Yes, I did, but I wanted to switch to English." I said.

"Why?" Sohila said.

"Because, I can make an easy living with English and there aren't many jobs in physics." I said.

"How can you make a living with English?" Sohila said.

"If you have a good technical background, and I do, you can make a lot of money as a technical writer."

"I never heard of a technical writer." Sohila said. "What do they do?"

"Technical writers write all the books people use to find out how to operate everything from tape players to rocket ships." I said.

"What have you written about?" Soraya said.

"I've written technical manuals about the hydraulic systems, electrical systems and pneumatic systems for aircraft, trucks, heavy equipment, mining equipment and power stations; I've also written about radio-controlled and computer-controlled equipment."

Ten Months in Iran

"But, you're a helicopter pilot. Why were you writing about mining equipment?" Soraya said.

"I graduated from the Vickers Hydraulic School in Troy, Michigan. Once you've mastered the basics of hydraulics, you can analyze and describe any system." I said.

"Have you ever been in California?" Soraya said.

"Yes, I have, many times." I said.

"Is it as wonderful as everyone says?" Soraya said.

"I was never anyplace I would classify as wonderful. But there probably are places that I would consider wonderful if I looked around long enough. I think anyone who tells you that a place is wonderful is giving you a subjective evaluation. What you think is wonderful, I might not see as wonderful; what I see as wonderful, Sohila may not see as wonderful."

"So, where were you and why didn't you like it?" Soraya said.

"I've been in San Diego, Los Angeles and San Francisco. They were too crowded, too expensive and too polluted." I said.

"Did you ever see any movie stars?" Soraya said.

"No, not in California, but I've seen movie stars in Vietnam and the Atlanta and Chicago airports. Everyone thinks you can go to California and see movie stars, but ninety nine percent of the people who live in California never see a movie star during their entire life."

"Oh, who have you seen?" Sohila said.

"I've seen Bob Hope, Ann Margaret, Roy Rogers, Boris Karloff, Lon Chaney, Bela Lugosi and Tex Ritter; the last four died when you were still just a baby."

"I know Bob Hope, Ann Margaret and Roy Rogers; I've seen them in movies." Sohila said.

"I would still like to go to California." Soraya said.

"Are you going to live in Ohio when you go back to the United States?" Sohila said.

Ten Months in Iran

"No, I'm going to go back to Fort Lauderdale, Florida. I have a daughter living there."

"Is Florida a wonderful place to you?" Soraya said.

"Yes, it is. I like warm weather and I love the ocean; I like sailing and SCUBA diving."

"I've never seen the ocean." Sohila said. "I did see the English channel when we went to London from Paris on the train[8]."

"Have you ever been to Paris or London?" Soraya said.

"Yes, I've been to both Paris and London. I love London, it's my favorite city."

"Did you like Paris?" Soraya said.

"I liked Paris, the Eiffel tower, the Louve museum, Notre Dame and especially French food. The only thing I didn't like about Paris was, too many Frenchmen." I said.

My comment about too many Frenchmen in Paris caused a look of bewilderment to envelop both Soraya and Sohila as they tried to translate my absurd statement into something meaningful. I finally had to explain to them that it was an old American joke. I told them that most Americans who travel to Paris come back complaining that the French are rude. Soraya surprised me with her comment that she also found them to be rude because, she said, they made fun of her French when they thought she couldn't hear them talking.

"What business is your father in?" Soraya said.

"My father is retired; the only thing he does is work in his garden and collect stamps." I said.

"What did he do before he retired?" She said.

"Dad quit school in the sixth grade and went to work as a carpenter to help support his family and worked as a

---

[8] At the time of this story, the train was broken up into short sections and placed on a ferry in France and taken off the ferry in England and reassembled to complete the journey.

Ten Months in Iran

carpenter most of his life. As a boy he started out as a framing carpenter and in just a few years, with his father's help, worked his way up to become a skilled cabinet maker. He had his own construction company for about ten years, but his partner wasn't much of a business man and squandered away their profits. After that he went to work at the Air Force station in Heath, first as a guard and then as a machinist. That was his last full time job."

About thirty minutes after we had finished eating Soraya produced a plate of cucumbers, cut up pomegranates and nuts for an after dinner snack. Later in the evening Soraya expressed a great deal of excitement over a new American portable sewing machine that she had just purchased so I told her that I would like to see it. She placed the machine on the rug and plugged it into an outlet. She told me that she hadn't used it yet and wanted to know if I knew anything about sewing machines. I told her that I did indeed know something about sewing machines and that I had made a graduation dress for my daughter Mary Linda. She was astounded and said she had never known a man who could sew except for professional tailors. She wanted to know if I could teach her how to sew and I said that I'd be happy to and that we could start right then. She acted like a young school girl who had just received a new doll. She jumped up and ran to get some material from another room. We spent the next hour and a half practicing how to make seams, borders and button holes. She couldn't seem to get over the fact that I enjoyed spending my time teaching two women to sew. Both ladies were extremely bright and handy because I saw things later that they had made and I never had to give them another lesson.

Before the evening was over I asked to return the favor by taking them to the Kourosh hotel nightclub for supper. They accepted and we made plans to meet at the hotel the next evening.

Ten Months in Iran

I Love Flying Cobras

I loved my job in Iran for several reasons, but the main one was that I flew Cobras and I flew alone. Pilots who flew helicopters that had a longer range and carried passengers had to take an Iranian security guard with them. I guess this was supposed to keep the pilot from stealing the aircraft because most of the Hueys could hold enough fuel to escape from the country. My Cobra, on the other hand, would fly for only about four hours or four hundred kilometers and since I was near the center of Iran the chance of making it to a secure area weren't too good.

I met another Cobra pilot on the flightline when he asked me for some help to determine whether or not the tail rotor links on the Cobra he was to fly that day were within tolerance. I told him that I was an inspector and would be happy to give him some help. After looking at the links I told him not to fly the aircraft because the tolerance was too close to the cutoff value. Since anyone could override his logbook write up, I wrote up the problem and signed my name to the entry to ground the aircraft. My signature forced a quality control man to check the links and it gave Mahmoud authority to request another aircraft. He thanked me for my help.

I enjoyed teaching pilots and their enlisted ground crew members about safety and the physics of how a helicopter actually managed to fly. It was more difficult to teach the enlisted men than the officers because the officers were all well trained in English. Many had gone to school in either England or the United States. The enlisted men were limited to the eight hundred word vocabulary that Tim was teaching in his night classes and therefore I was also limited to that vocabulary. I had to consult his list of

Ten Months in Iran

words when I made up my lesson plans for each class. I had to really be careful not to let my classes degenerate into an English class because they all wanted so much to learn to speak better English.

It was during my safety classes that I found out that the pilots and ground crew members believed that the date of their death was already written down in Allah's book. Their standard answer when cautioned about taking chances in traffic or in the air was "When Allah calls me, I will go." Iranians were great at memorizing things and you'd think that capacity would be a terrific asset when they were required to memorize aircraft emergency procedures. I soon learned that memorizing the words without understanding the underlying purpose was of no value whatsoever.

In fact, I found out that it was actually a detriment because when they were presented with a simulated emergency they would start from the beginning and recite all the procedures in their head until they got to the relevant solution. Obviously, when you have only a fraction of a second to respond to an emergency, this approach doesn't work. American pilots memorize the actions required for a particular emergency and often have difficulty reciting the text that covers the procedure. I think the root of the Iranian's problem can be traced to their approach to religion. Many of the Islamic countries promote and some even require young boys to memorize passages from the Qur'an; so they are familiar with rote memorization from an early age. The Qur'an presents many rules for everyday life that are still valid today and it outlines what could be, if followed, a beautiful religion. However, just like emergency procedures, memorizing the text does not mean you understand the concept.

Ten Months in Iran
Sex and the Single Male

On the day my first in-country check flight was scheduled, I arrived early to preflight the aircraft.

One of the American plane captains called to me as I was walking out to the aircraft. He wanted me to look at something he'd found in the brush just off the flight line. The item of interest was a lean-to that some Iranian troops had constructed as a place to hide during the day either to get out of the sun or to get out of work. I told him that soldiers all over the world were the same, if they could figure out a way to get out of work they'd do it. He told me that I was missing the point! He told me to get down and look inside; so, I got down and looked inside but didn't see anything unusual. Then he told me to lie down and look up. When I did, I saw what he was talking about. Attached to the roof of the lean-to was a life-size, full color picture of a naked man.

I found out that homosexuality was rampant in Iran, and I think at least part of the problem can be traced to two basic causes: nature and Islam. Nature contributes her part by releasing a flood of hormones when a boy reaches a certain age. This rush of hormones compels him to seek a mate and to try and reproduce, so the boy starts looking for a female. Then Islamic custom and law, in all of its infinite wisdom, contributes its input to the tragedy. Islam not only hides the female, it forbids looking at, touching, smelling or talking to the female. So, where can all this sexual energy go? Where can this irresistible and natural force be directed? It can only be directed towards other boys who are having the same crises or older men who have accepted it as a way of life.

However, if a boy (or man) should find a female who is alone and cooperative (or not cooperative) and has sex with her, then the female is punished (possibly killed by her relatives if they are really hard core Islamists) for tarnishing the family name. The boy is not punished. In order for the boy to be punished by Islamic law there must be three male witnesses to the encounter (or rape).

If a young boy and a girl are just caught alone they are automatically accused of having sex and the girl could be forced to take a virginity test to prove that nothing happened. Under these less severe circumstances a boy could be forced to marry a girl if, after being examined by a doctor, she is found not to be a virgin or if she becomes pregnant.

The Iranian attitude toward sex is evidenced by their popular saying that 'when a man and a woman are alone, the devil is the third person in the room'. They use this saying as evidence that something has happened even though there were no witnesses because theoretically the devil was the witness. If a woman is married and caught in a compromising situation with another man the man can be publicly flogged and the woman stoned to death.

Maggie Changes Her Rules

Maggie came in on me as I was changing my clothes in the pilot's locker room.

"Jack, I haven't seen you around for awhile. Where have you been?" she said.

"I've been busy." I said.

"I've been thinking about my rule about never going out with the same man twice and I think I would like to break that rule with you. What do you think about the idea?" she said.

"I wish you had decided to break that rule a few weeks earlier." I said.

"Why?"

Ten Months in Iran

"Because I'm going with an Iranian girl now and I'm really serious about her."

"Oh, my god, Jack," she said, "you're not going to marry an Iranian girl who's never seen her own pussy, are you? If she's never seen it do you think she's going to let you see it?"

"What the hell are you talking about?" I said.

"Iranian women, they don't bathe and they don't fuck in the nude." she said.

"Where did you hear that?" I said.

"From Iranian men I've known, I've been told that fundamentalist Muslims don't ever see their body nude. When they bathe and when they fuck, they wear a white cotton night shirt that goes clear to their knees." she said.

"How can you wash with something like that on?" I said.

"They wash up under it when they bathe and the man has to wear one too when they make love. And, oh yes, they're supposed to be under the covers when they have sex. The man isn't supposed to see her tits or her pussy either."

"You're making this up." I said.

"No, I'm not. I've been with Iranian men who've told me that Iranians never lay together naked like we do."

"Well, some fanatic Muslims may behave that way but I don't think all of them go to that extreme." I said.

"Don't say I didn't warn you. Let me know what happens the first time you try to get in her pants."

"Well, unless invited, I've no intention of trying to get into her pants until I find out where our relationship is going. Besides, I couldn't do it even if I wanted to because her sister is always with us."

The Check Flight

Another reason that I loved my job in Iran was that I had a one hundred square mile area that was reserved for test

Ten Months in Iran

flights and there weren't that many test pilots. Consequently, I mostly had the area to myself. The area was ten miles by ten miles by two miles high and that gave me two hundred cubic miles of air to play in. It was like being in heaven for a pilot. The helicopters I tested were AH-1J Cobras, a much improved two-engine model of the AH-1G Cobra that I flew in Vietnam.

After preflighting the aircraft I sat down on the skid and waited for the instructor pilot to arrive. He wanted to go over the preflight again with me to see how much I knew about the aircraft's components. Since the Cobra was really the only helicopter that I had ever flown extensively - I had 1600 hours in the Cobra and I was a qualified maintenance officer and test pilot - I knew things about the Cobra that he didn't know. It wasn't long before he said that he thought I was completely familiar with the Cobra and that we could proceed with the check flight. During my check flight he gave me a simulated stuck tail rotor emergency. I had a real stuck tail rotor emergency in Vietnam and handled it successfully, so I was confident that I could handle it again without any problem. As I approached the runway I slowed the aircraft down and was flying down the runway at an altitude of about three feet, the nose of the helicopter was about thirty degrees to the right of the center line of the runway. As the aircraft slowed and started to sink, I cut the power and the nose came around to the center line of the runway as I touched down.

"Jesus, Jack!" He said. "That was beautiful! However, we aren't supposed to do touchdown maneuvers during training. So, don't tell anyone about what you just did."

He told me that all simulated emergencies were to be recovered at three feet. I asked him how a pilot is supposed to master an emergency procedure if he can't take it all the way to the ground. I told him that mastering

Ten Months in Iran

the last three feet was where the emergency was really solved. He told me that he didn't agree with the policy but he could only follow orders. Then he told me that we were supposed to do three stuck tail rotor emergencies but considering how I took care of the first one he would skip the other two.

We took off and headed out towards the desert for the next phase of my flight check. As we were flying I saw the power indicator lights on the automatic flight stabilization system (SCAS) go out, so I knew what the next test was. He was trying to see if I could fly the Cobra without the flight stabilization system. He was quiet for awhile and I could see the SCAS power lights go back on and then back off again. Finally he asked me if the power lights on the SCAS were off. I told him yes, they're off. I've turned the SCAS on and off while you have been flying and I can't tell the difference. I started laughing and then told him that I had been a test pilot for about five years and that I made most of my test flights with the SCAS off. Otherwise, I told him, you can't tell what's wrong with the aircraft if you have the flight stabilization system on because it covers up small control problems. Again, he was quiet for awhile and then told me to just fly around for awhile and have some fun. Your check flight's over. I asked him if he had ever done a barrel roll in a Cobra and he said that he hadn't and that he really didn't want to, so I dropped the subject.

That evening at home I was very excited about my date with Sohila. I had no idea why a beautiful young lady like Sohila would be attracted to me but I was so happy that she was. I got ready to meet the ladies as fast as I could because I would have to walk to the hotel, Tim had the car.

Ten Months in Iran

As I was walking there, I saw the strangest sight. At first I couldn't make out what was going on; a man in a business suit was down on both knees facing a wall about five meters back in an alleyway. Now, when I say facing, I mean close; his nose was almost touching the wall. Finally it came to me, he's taking a leak! I couldn't wait to talk to someone about what I had just seen. In the lobby of the hotel I met Mahmoud Taheri, the pilot I had helped earlier in the day. I knew he had been in Iran for a long time so I asked him.

He told me that an Iranian's idea of a public toilet is to seek relief in a side street. However, they had to be careful not to urinate towards Mecca or to urinate on a wall. It's against Islamic law to urinate towards Mecca or to urinate on a wall. To insure that they don't urinate towards Mecca, many Iranian men have a pocket-watch-like device that always tells them the direction to Mecca. And, to avoid urinating on a wall they get down on their knees and urinate into the crack between the wall and the pavement (if the street is paved). If urinating in a back street that was not paved they still performed the same maneuver and don't ask me how they do it without getting their knees wet.

I told him that I understood then why the first ten meters of every alley I've ever walked into reeked with the smell of urine.

I waited in the lobby until the ladies arrived so they wouldn't have to walk into the nightclub unescorted. They arrived dressed in modern western clothes and they both looked beautiful. You had only to see Soraya walk into a room (or a hotel lobby) to be aware of how bold and confident she was with her status in society. I knew that being a widow and an older woman gave her a certain amount of immunity from the scrutiny younger women had to endure; and the fact that she was from a wealthy and educated family, I think, also gave her a bold

Ten Months in Iran

confidence that the poor and under educated didn't have. If she had any apprehension about walking into the hotel without an escort, it didn't show. Sohila, on the other hand, didn't act all that confident; it looked like she was stuck to her sister after they got out of the taxi.

I met them at the door and we took the elevator to the club. I already had made arrangements with the maitre d to seat us next to the dance floor where the entertainment was to take place later in the evening. Sometimes it amazed me what an American ten dollar bill could do for you in Iran. We were given a center table on the edge of the dance floor and the maitre d kept checking on us all through the evening to make sure we were being given special care. I was trying to impress Sohila and Soraya, but we received such attention that I was impressed.

We were at the Kourosh for about four hours eating and dancing. Soraya and I had some wine; Sohila didn't drink. I danced with both ladies and some of the unattached older men in the club danced with Soraya. I thought Soraya had probably been at the nightclub before by the way she acted and she seemed to be familiar with the layout, she knew where the ladies room was. Sohila, on the other hand, seemed a little uncomfortable at first but after we had eaten and danced a few times she began to relax. The entertainer was a young French woman who sang songs in Farsi, French and English and, of course, Sohila could understand and enjoy all of them. Sohila was impressed with the singer and her ability to sing in Farsi, which she said was not an easy task for a foreigner to master.

We were joined later in the evening by Mahmoud, Tom Mix and his girlfriend Farah. Tom and Farah were young, intelligent and good looking, the type of young people

Ten Months in Iran

you liked to see together. I could tell by the way they looked at each other that they were in love. I knew his job as a senior quality control inspector with Bell paid well. And I knew, after talking with him, that he was sending a good deal of it to a bank in the states, so he would be a good husband and provider for her. She was a beautiful young Iranian girl of about nineteen or twenty who had a job in Bell's public relations department. I was intrigued by the fact that she was there without a chaperone.

"Farah," I said. "how did you get your position with Bell?"

"Nepotism," she said, "my aunt Mariam is a manager in the section that handles hiring Iranian help."

"What does you family think about you working for Bell?"

"They don't know anything about it; my family lives in the city of Zahedan located in the Southeast corner of Iran near the borders of Pakistan and Afghanistan. I live here with my aunt where I work and go to university. If my father knew about it, I would be locked up just like all the other young Iranian girls."

I wasn't going to touch that comment and was really searching for a way to change the subject. As silence fell over the table, I think Soraya saw the predicament I had gotten myself into and took control.

"You're lucky," Soraya said, "to have an aunt who is not only progressive enough, but also has sufficient self confidence to help you escape from some of our archaic customs."

"We're both lucky." Sohila said. "You have your aunt and I have my sister; otherwise we would both be walking around in the dark."

"I'm a Muslim." Mahmoud said. "However, we in America practice Islam and follow the Qur'an without all the Arab induced cultural taboos."

Ten Months in Iran

I knew where Mahmoud was going with his statement. The Iranians think of themselves as Persians and it irritates them when anyone refers to them as Arabs. So, stating that he was a Muslim and distancing himself from Arabs and their ancient customs went over well with the ladies at the table.

After we had been sitting around the table and talking for some time it became apparent that Mahmoud was interested in Soraya and that she was interested in him. That was a break for me because he took her to another table so they could talk, and when Tom and Farah danced, Sohila and I were alone to talk. She told me that she had never been truly alone with a man before, that her sister had always been in the room. Even when she was in school in Paris her sister was there to chaperone her every move. We talked about the Islamic custom of wearing a chador.

"Soraya and I do not like to wear the chador because it's uncomfortable and makes us sweat and sweat ruins your clothing. Soraya doesn't normally wear a chador anyway because she is older and has been married. However, she always has one handy just in case I need it. I always wear one when I go to the gold bazaar because the bazaar is a stronghold of the religious zealots and they get a great deal of pleasure out of tormenting young girls."

"How do they torment you?"

"They're rude to you, call you names and won't wait on you. There have been occasions where they've gotten physical with women who wouldn't passively accept their abuse." She said.

"What do you mean by physical?"

"Well, they have grabbed women and thrown them out of their shops." she said.

"Didn't the Shah's father decree twenty years ago that Iranian women no longer had to wear the chador?" I said.

Ten Months in Iran

"Yes, he did, but the mullahs are still pushing it during their Friday sermons and causing young girls who choose not to wear one a lot of problems and humiliation. Many of the young women I know say that it's easier to wear the chador than it is to put up with the trouble. I just have to watch what areas of the city I go into when I'm not wearing one." she said.

She told me she considered herself a good Muslim and then qualified the statement by adding 'as defined by her father'. I took this statement to mean that her father also had some reservations about the Islamic culture. I felt an emotional attraction to Sohila that I hadn't felt for anyone for a long time. She was beautiful, intelligent and ten years below the cutoff age of women I could usually tolerate. As we got ready to leave, Mahmoud insisted on paying for Soraya's portion of the tab. Once in the lobby, Mahmoud and Soraya went off into a corner to talk leaving Sohila and me alone again.

"I had a wonderful time tonight and I'd like to take you out again." I said.

"I also had a good time and I would like to see you again." She said.

Mahmoud and I walked them out to the taxi and split the fare to send them home.

"Thank you, Soraya, for having supper with me and for allowing me to enjoy the company of your sister." I said. "This was such an enjoyable evening."

"You're welcome, Jack." Soraya said. "I'm sure Sohila also enjoyed your company."

After the ladies left, I exchanged phone numbers with Mahmoud and told him that I would call and let him know when we were going to get together again.

Ten Months in Iran
Help for Christina

On Saturday I picked up Christina and took her to breakfast at the hotel before cleaning the house. She still acted more like a boy than a young girl. She ate too fast, talked with food in her mouth and had poor table manners in general. She was a good worker though. We would work side by side cleaning the house and she never let me do more than she had done. We would get hot and sweaty cleaning the house because the air conditioner was off while the doors were open to hose out the rooms.

On this particular day, as we were sitting on my couch taking a Coke break from cleaning she let a ripping fart and then vigorously laughed about it. I didn't laugh; I gave her a disappointed look and moved away from her. At that point, I thought it was time for me to introduce her to some role models that would allow her to see how ladies were supposed to act. I decided to start taking her along occasionally with Soraya and Sohila to the nightclub at the hotel and to restaurants to eat lunch and supper. I made up my mind to talk to her mother about my plan the next time I saw her.

After we finished cleaning the house we cleaned ourselves up and went to the Korean restaurant for lunch. During lunch I started talking to her about how important good manners and proper English were in determining the degree of success you enjoy during your life. I told her that my father only went to the sixth grade and that he worked in a Southern Ohio coal mine during his youth. He escaped to a somewhat better life because he was an excellent carpenter.

I also told her that my mother was a West Virginia McCoy and that mom and dad were married when she was sixteen. I explained to her that during my youth I was taught the basic values that made America strong - honor, honesty, hard work and fair play and that when I was

Ten Months in Iran

young I always thought that dad was a success. We had a house and a car, we were never hungry and I had clothes and shoes. Until I went into the Navy I thought I knew everything I needed to know to be a success.

"Christina," I said, "I wasn't in the navy long before I knew I was missing something. I looked at what I was doing and then I looked at what the officers were doing and asked … why? The first answer I got was: education. So, I started out on a long journey; I took every technical education course the Navy offered and completed every Navy school I could get. I started moving up through the ranks very quickly and soon became aware of another requirement for success: English.

The Navy started grading its petty officers on their ability to communicate and that grade, along with your technical ability, controlled your promotions. Once again, I started out on another long journey; I completed every English course the Navy education center had and then started taking English courses at the local college. After twelve years as an enlisted man in the Navy I became a Signal Corps Officer in the United States Army. I didn't stop studying though, and by the time I got out of the Army I had racked up seven years of college."

"I'm going to go to college." she said.

"Yes, I know. Your dad told me that your aunt has already put up the money to send you to college in Hawaii where she lives. But, you shouldn't wait until you get to college to start working on your English and your social skills."

"What do you mean by social skills?"

"Christina," I said, "social skills, or the lack of social skills, will determine how you interact with other people and they control how other people react towards you. If you have good social skills people will like you. If you have poor social skills, people will think you're crude and will probably not want to be around you." I said.

"Do I have poor social skills?" she said.

Ten Months in Iran

"Honey," I said, "let's just say that your social skills need a little work."
"Is that why you moved away from me today?"
"Yes."
"Will you help me?"
"Yes."

A Persian Rug for Mom

The next day I went to the bazaar for the sole purpose of buying my mother a Persian rug. I wasn't in a hurry so I walked through all the shops to see which one had a rug that I thought mom would like. I could close my eyes and visualize mom's house so I knew what would match and what would clash with the way she had decorated it. I selected a shop and walked in; the shop owner was either very hungry for a sale or I just looked like an easy target because he was all over me as soon as I stepped inside. He was pulling out rugs and throwing them around the floor and telling me how much better his rugs were than the rugs in the other shops. He was showing me how close together the weave was and that he used better material than anyone else. He never shut up from the time I walked in until I pointed to a rug that I was interested in. Oh, he exclaimed. I had picked the best rug in his shop and that I must really know rugs to have picked out that one. I asked him how much he wanted for the rug and he told me $500.00 American dollars. I laughed at him and dug into my pocket and pulled out a Kennedy half dollar and offered it to him. At that point he grabbed me by the arm and threw me out of his shop. But he continued to negotiate outside by coming down to $400.00 American dollars.

I made a counter offer of $20.00 and he again became irate and tried to push me down the alley away from his

97

Ten Months in Iran

shop; still negotiating, He came down to $300.00 American dollars. I made another counter offer of $30.00; this time he didn't get irate with me but immediately came down to $100.00 American dollars. I shook my head like I wasn't satisfied and started to walk away. He took my arm and pulled me back and asked me what I would offer. I gave him $50.00 dollars and took the rug home. I probably could have gotten the rug for $40.00 dollars but I started feeling sorry for the guy.

Tom and Farah

It was a Saturday night and I didn't have a date with Sohila, so I decided to pick up Christina and take her out for a pizza. Tom and Farah walked in as we were eating our pizza.
"Tom," I said, "over here."
"Well, I see you've found the only pizza shop in Isfahan that makes a pizza that actually tastes like a pizza." he said.
"Yes, we come here often." I said. "This is Christina. She's the daughter of a friend of mine."
"How do you do, Christina?" Tom said. "This is Farah."
Farah sat down with us while Tom went up to the window to order their pizza.
"How do you like Iran, Christina?" Farah said.
"I like it a lot more now that Jack takes me out every week and pays me to clean his place on Saturdays." she said. "Before I met Jack, I was stuck at home seven days a week with my little brother and I had no money."
"Are you getting acquainted with everyone, honey?" Tom said, as he delivered their pizza.
"Yes, Christina and I are having a nice conversation." Farah said. "It seems like Jack has saved her from a life of boredom during her stay here."
"Well, what do you do to ward off boredom?" he said.

Ten Months in Iran

"He takes me to the nightclub at the Kourosh hotel; on weekends, we eat breakfast at the Kourosh before I clean his house and then afterwards he takes me to the Korean restaurant for lunch." she said.

"You clean his house to fight off boredom?" he said.

"No, I clean his house because he pays me." she said.

I was anxious to get away from that topic so I made an effort to change the focus of the conversation.

"What plans do you two have?" I said.

"I'm saving up all the money I can so we can go to the states and be married." He said.

"I thought you were going to go to college when you got back."

"I am, the government is going to pay for most of that." he said.

"When is all this going to happen?"

"I think I'll have enough money saved up in four to five months."

"Are you excited about going to the United States, Farah?" I said.

"Yes, I am. I've always wanted to visit the United States; now, I'll be living there." she said.

"What do you think your parents are going to say about you marring an infidel?" I said.

"By the time they find out, it will be too late to say anything about it."

"Well, I hope the two of you are being very careful and not telling a lot of people about your plans" I said.

"Actually, no one knows about our plans except her aunt Mariam and you." Tom said.

"What does your aunt think about the plan?" I said.

"She has agreed to help us." She said.

The remainder of the evening was relatively quiet as we sat and ate our pizza. I had some reservations about their plan; I have always believed that the only way to keep a secret is not to tell anyone.

Ten Months in Iran
Crown Prince Reza Pahlavi Base
Army Airfield

During my Monday morning class I received a notice alerting me to the unsafe practices of some of our Iranian pilots who were in training. The warning was about flying too low to the ground in the desert and too low over water. I warned my class that flying too close to a uniform surface that does not have objects on its surface that can be seen and recognized at one hundred knots is extremely dangerous. The problem is that you can't tell how far away you are from a uniform or slick surface and you can easily fly into it. It might be fun to fly close to the desert to see how much of a rooster tail you can kick up at one hundred knots but it will eventually kill you. It was only a few weeks later that two Iranian Cobra pilots were killed when they flew their aircraft into the Zayandeh River. Witnesses said the aircraft was flying very fast and very low to the water. We never found out if they had flown into the river because they misjudged their altitude or if they had had an engine failure and crashed due to poor emergency procedures. I told our pilots that high speed and low altitude is a deadly combination. I warned them that if they had an engine failure at high speed and low altitude they would most likely die because a Cobra's nose will tuck down during a high speed engine failure and that they didn't have a lot of time to figure out what to do about it; they had to immediately pull the nose up or die.

I was talking to Mahmoud about Iranian pilots and asked him what his opinion was. He told me that they had a definite lack of respect for safety procedures. He said that he had twenty student pilots and that two of them were killed in traffic accidents and that four were killed in aircraft accidents that were either caused by not being

Ten Months in Iran

able to execute their emergency procedures in a timely manner or by just taking stupid chances. Mahmoud expressed amazement at the ideas and beliefs of the Iranians. He had no idea where their ideas or beliefs come from but said they didn't come for the Qur'an. He had been a Muslim all of his life and had read and studied the Qur'an ever since he was old enough to read. But, he told me the Iranians didn't consider him a true Muslim because he was an American.

"I read a verse from the Qur'an and it means one thing to me; they read the same verse and it means something totally different to them. They're just like the Southern crackers that'll hate me until the day I die because their parents taught them to be prejudiced. The Iranians will hate Jews and Christians until the day they die because the mullahs have taught them to be prejudiced. When you're taught something from birth it will be with you until death."

"Mahmoud, I never knew you were so cynical." I said.

"Jack, you are just now being exposed to prejudice. I've been living with it all my life."

"Don't give me that 'you don't know what prejudice is' shit, Mahmoud. Americans have a lot bigger load of prejudices than just the color-of-your-skin prejudice. If you are born a true WASP[9], you're prejudiced against people who are too dark or too white, too poor or too rich, too educated or too un-educated, too tall or too short, too fat or too skinny and anyone who has a Southern accent, New York accent, European accent or a Latin accent. The only accents that are normally accepted in the United States without prejudice are an English accent or a Canadian accent as long as it isn't French Canadian. And, least I forget, WASPs do not like to socialize with Jews or Catholics."

---

[9] White Anglo-Saxon Protestant

Ten Months in Iran

"My god, Jack, you have the nerve to call me cynical."

"Let me tell you something, Mahmoud. When I was fourteen years old my father worked as a carpenter at Weekly Lumber Company. Dad got me a job cutting Mister Weekly's grass during the summer and while working there I meet his thirteen year old daughter who I thought was the most beautiful little thing God had ever placed on the earth. He either saw us talking or she said something about me to him because I was fired from cutting his grass and told that my family was poor and uneducated and that we would always be poor and uneducated and that I was not to see or talk to his daughter again.

I was so ashamed of the whole episode that I never told anyone what happened. And, you know, I have no idea how much that traumatic episode has had in affecting the choices that I've had to make during my life. I often wonder if that episode hadn't happened, would I be someone else today? So, you see, Mahmoud, we all have psychological loads to carry and every load is heavy to the person who has it on his back."

"I'm sorry, Jack. I know that when I was young I thought white people always got every thing they wanted. However, I think the first close white friend that I had in collage made that myth evaporate."

"Mahmoud, the world is absolutely full of myths. Don't feel bad because you have fallen for one or more of them. I believe all this bullshit about religion is the biggest myth mankind has ever fallen for." I said.

"Jack, I know you're not too religious but do you really believe that it's all bullshit?"

"Yes, I believe its all bullshit. Bullshit started by someone primarily to relieve primal anxieties and later used to control people. I can't believe, after all our talks about religion, that I haven't told you my story about how religion started."

Ten Months in Iran

"No, Jack, you've never told me the story; but I'm sure I'm going to hear it now."

Well, if you really want to hear it, this is the way it goes; I call the story *The Birth of God*."

Mahmoud settled back, folded his arms across his chest and had a rather skeptical look on his face as I started my story.

"Somewhere back in time when people were just developing into conscious beings, a group of people were huddled in a cave and terrified by a raging storm. In an effort to calm the group, a woman, who was not as terrified as the others, told a story. The story was her explanation about what was causing all the water to fall from the sky, the loud noises, the flashing light that momentarily turned the night into day and the frightening fingers of light from the sky that poked the ground and started fires. The storyteller told the group of a great being who lived in the sky and who ruled over all the earth. The storyteller continued to explain that the great being was angry about something that had taken place that day and was in a rage. She then assured them that they hadn't done anything wrong that day so the great being's anger must be aimed at another tribe and that they were safe in their cave.

Since men were known to become angry over the smallest event and then destroy everything in a fit of rage, it was not long until the group decided that the great being she had told them about had to be a man.

Soon, mothers found out that they could get their children to do what they wanted them to do by saying 'the great being will be angry if you don't do what I say.' Then, after the storyteller died and the story became accepted as true, a man discovered that he could control the entire group by telling them 'the great being will be angry if you don't do what I say.'

Ten Months in Iran

Not long after this discovery, every event (desirable or undesirable) was attributed to the great being's state of satisfaction and, in the case of undesirable events, someone had to take the blame; someone had to be sacrificed to appease the great being.

Today, after hundreds of thousands years of trying to appease the great being, man has developed an amazing array of ideas and methods of controlling people by telling them 'the great being will be angry if you don't do what I say.'

But, you know what really amazes me, Mahmoud? Is how this one story, told somewhere in a cave in Africa could have developed into the more than three thousand different religions that exist today. All of these religions adamantly claim to be based on a benevolent god, but their followers are dedicated to killing anyone who believes in any of the other 2999 religions."

Mahmoud looked at me for a long time shaking his head.

"Jack, I wish I had a comeback for that. But, I don't. It may very well be true. The only thing I can say is that it doesn't take into account any possible divine intervention."

After I left Mahmoud, I ran into Jay.

"Have you heard about Tom and Farah?" he said.

"No, what happened?" I said.

"Farah's family heard about her having a job with Bell and about her having an American boyfriend. Her father sent her uncle here to get her and take her back home. When the uncle got here he threatened to kill her boyfriend if he could find him. Neither Farah nor Mariam would tell him where Tom lived or his name so he severely beat both of them. I didn't see Farah, but I did see Mariam and she looked like shit. He really worked her over."

"Did they ever give him a name?"

Ten Months in Iran

"No, and luckily, they never told the neighbors his name because he questioned them. They knew what he looked like but didn't know his name."

"How is Tom taking this?"

"Not good, I'm afraid." he said. "Not only is he devastated by the loss of Farah, Bell is sending him home because they're afraid his identity will be discovered and that he will be killed."

"So, he's losing out all the way around."

"Yes, he is. He loved her so much and she loved him. They were planning to go to the states to get married. They waited too long."

"How could a young girl like that get out of the country?" I said.

"Mariam was going to take her out of the country on vacation and then just not bring her back." he said.

"That's a moot point now."

"Do you have any idea how they found out about them?" I said.

"No, I don't."

Trouble with the Guards

I left the training facility the next day to drive over to the airfield for a test flight. In the parking lot I found my car blocked in by another car, double parked behind me. I could not get out by going forward because there was a tree in front of me so I used my car to push the other car back far enough to let me out. Two Iranian soldiers standing guard in the parking lot told me to go with them to see their Colonel about what I had done.

At the Colonel's office the two soldiers related the story to the Colonel, who then told them to return to the parking lot. He asked me if I'd pushed the other car out of the way and I said that I had. He asked me why and I told him that

Ten Months in Iran

I had no choice. I had a tree directly in front of me and the car was double parked behind me. I had to push it out of the way so I could get to the airfield to flight test a helicopter. He told me that he would have to keep me there for a few minutes so his soldiers would think that he was giving me hell for what I'd done and asked me if I would like to have some tea.

I noticed that he had American jump wings on his uniform and asked him if he'd gone through jump school at Fort Benning, Georgia. He told me he had and then I told him that I was also an airborne graduate from Benning and that I'd also been a Green Beret in Vietnam. We drank tea and talked for some time about our experiences in jump school. After that meeting Colonel Amir Abdul Ehya and I became good friends and I visited him often to talk about our common experiences and he also loved to hear my war stories about Vietnam.

Saying Good Bye to Tom

I saw Tom walking across the tarmac and ran over to talk to him and see how he was holding up under the stress of losing his girl and his job on the same day.

"Tom, wait up." I said.

He stopped and turned to see who was calling him. As I walked up to him he didn't look at me but looked at the ground. He was a mess; his clothes weren't pressed and he looked like he hadn't shaved in a few days. After seeing him, I decided not to ask how he was holding up because it was apparent from his looks; he was not holding up well at all.

"I heard about your misfortune Tom. I'm so sorry. I wish there was something I could do to help; but, I know there isn't anything anyone can say or do to relieve your pain."

"Thanks, anyway, Jack." he said. "I appreciate you concern."

Ten Months in Iran

"When are you going home?"

"My flight leaves tonight." he said.

"I wish things could've turned out differently for you, Tom." I said. "I'll miss seeing you around here."

We shook hands, said good bye and walked off in different directions.

Cobra Crash

That afternoon while I was waiting in the hangar for the mechanics to complete their work on an aircraft I was scheduled to test fly, I heard a terrific noise outside the hangar. It sounded like someone stuck a very large plank into an even larger fan. Several of us ran outside to see what was causing the noise. What we saw was a hovering Cobra that was out of control; it was swinging back and forth like a pendulum until the rotor blade hit the ground and the helicopter started spinning around violently to the right. Now it was completely out of control; it bounced two or three times before falling over onto its right side and ripping the transmission loose. Pieces of the aircraft's rotor blade were flying through the air and falling to the ground everywhere. As soon as the activity stopped we ran over to help the pilots out. Neither pilot was injured - one was an American IP[10], the other an Iranian student.

The accident investigation board learned that the aircraft's automatic flight stabilization (SCAS) system had gone bad and was sending error signals to the controls. The instructor pilot, in the front seat, turned the power off to the stabilization system but the problem didn't stop and he couldn't gain control of the aircraft. The board found out that the power off switch for the stabilization system didn't actually cut all the power to the system. Not long

---

[10] Instructor Pilot

after that accident we received new emergency procedures that called for pulling the circuit breakers if a stabilization problem was encountered.

Flying in the Desert

Early one morning as I was checking in I was given an assignment to pick up a Cobra that had been abandoned at a remote airfield. I was flown to the airfield in a Bell 205. An Iranian pilot had put the Cobra down because he was having trouble flying it without a working automatic flight stabilization (SCAS) system. Since I performed a great deal of my flight tests with the SCAS system turned off, its malfunction made little difference to me. I pulled the circuit breakers on the system to eliminate any chance of it kicking in and out during the flight and started back to Isfahan. There was absolutely no problem with the aircraft except the SCAS system. The Cobra was armed. It was the first time I had flown an armed helicopter in Iran and it was a little heaver than usual. I was surprised that the aircraft was armed because there were no firing ranges in this area Southeast of Isfahan. My second thought was that they were having some trouble on either the Afghanistan border or the Pakistani border. I inspected the aircraft for bullet holes and found none.

I served as the co-pilot during the flight out to the airfield so I had a good deal of time to look out the window at the countryside. We flew over several small settlements and villages and I noticed that nearly each one had an associated large deep hole close by and several hundreds of feet of pipe leading from small buildings to the inhabited areas. The pilot I was with told me that the pipes were carrying water to the villagers. He also told me that the large holes were part of an underground canal system called a qanat that was dug by the Persians, some of them hundreds of years ago.

Ten Months in Iran

The qanat system taps into the water table near the mountains and delivers it to the plains through large tunnels, some of which are three hundred feet under ground. He told me he had read stories about the men who dug the early canals being drowned when they broke through to the water table and about others being drowned digging tunnels designed to tap into an existing water-filled tunnel.

The little huts on the surface were pumping stations that delivered water to the settlements and villages that lay along the route of the qanat. He said the Bell 205 that he flew was like a desert pickup truck to the Iranians and that he often flew repair parts out to the pumping stations.

Female Soldiers

That evening as I was leaving the airbase, traffic was being held up at the gate by someone having difficulty with the guards. As I sat there I noticed female soldiers entering the guard house in uniform on the base side and exiting on the civilian side in chadors. I was confounded and totally amazed by what I was witnessing. This was one of those times that I actually felt that I had indeed slipped into the *Twilight Zone*. I was jerked out of my daze by the blast of a truck horn; I looked up and there were no longer any cars in front of me.

I couldn't get that image out of my head - it was like a ghost ship that would sail through my dreams at night and wake me up. It did, however, answer a question that I'd had for a long time and that was: why hadn't I ever seen a woman in uniform on the streets of Isfahan, considering there were hundreds of them on the base. How does a woman's psyche adjust to such a practice? How do they justify it to themselves? This was additional evidence to me that to live and survive as a Muslim in Iran you had to be schizophrenic. You had to have two different conflicting identities within you, one subjugated self and one free self and you had to know which one to let out on any given situation. Some of these women were sergeants and had real authority within the confines of the airbase. How could they adjust to becoming a subservient second-class citizen that must hide under a black sheet because they have passed through some invisible barrier as they pass beyond the perimeter of the air base?

I knew one female sergeant who was a jet engine mechanic and repair team crew chief. She had five or six men working for her. On the inside of the airbase she was the boss. Outside of the airbase, any one of her male workers could rape her and as long as there weren't three male witnesses, they couldn't be charged. As long as they didn't beat her up and make the attack obvious, she probably wouldn't tell anyone anyway because she wouldn't want the disgrace to get back to her family. Is it any wonder that the Shah wanted to drag Iran into the twentieth century and give women more of a say about their lives?

Mail Call

At 2 PM everyday I went to the main building to see if I had any mail. I received all of my mail on the airbase through Bell Helicopter's mail system. All letters and packages were delivered to the mail room close to my classroom. However, my outgoing mail was via the Iranian mail system. I received letters regularly from mom and dad and occasionally from my five daughters. I was sending money to my daughter Sue for college and rent for her apartment. On one occasion she needed some extra money for something and mailed a letter to my Iranian address to ask for it. But she put a regular stamp on the letter, like she was mailing it from Ohio to Georgia, and it

Ten Months in Iran

took two months for the letter to get to me. That letter must have crossed the Atlantic on a ship to England and then traveled by train to Isfahan. By the time I got the letter it was dirty from the trip and the reason she needed the money had passed. She was upset with me for a long time for not sending her the money in time for her emergency.

Care Packages

You didn't have to be in Iran long to know there were certain things that were not available in the stores. The number one all important item was toilet paper. Iran must have had some type of trade agreement with Russia to purchase all of their toilet paper from them because the only toilet paper available in the stores was Russian. The closest thing we have in the United States to Russian toilet paper is the waxed paper mothers used to wrap sandwiches with before plastic baggies were invented. The fact that it's waxed isn't the only problem; American toilet paper is four and a half inches wide, Russian toilet paper is only three inches wide. One of the first lessons you learn when using Russian toilet paper is that you do not crinkle it up in an attempt to make it do a better job. I could have started a black market in American toilet paper if I had just known ahead of time. After about six months, I did find a small market that had English toilet paper that I could buy to hold me over between care packages from home.

The second item that I could only get from home was a deodorant that actually worked. In a country where the summer time temperature reaches to 120^0 F, deodorant is an important item to have in your medicine cabinet. Europeans were not big on using deodorant and you only had to ride in an elevator with a group of them to

Ten Months in Iran

appreciate that fact. The Iranians, except those educated in the United States, thought the smell of a man's sweat actually turned a woman on sexually. I had several Iranian women tell me that it was an absurd idea, that it was a male Iranian myth and was definitely not true.

Another item that was really critical to me was razor blades. In a land where many of the men don't shave, razor blades weren't a hot item. And, I soon found out that the Russians weren't any better at making razor blades than they were at making toilet paper. I could only imagine that shaving with a Russian razor was like trying to shave with a piece of broken glass. Once again I was saved by the English when I found some razor blades at the same little market where I got the English toilet paper.

The last item on my care package request list was toothpaste. The European and Russian toothpaste wasn't bad but it wasn't American either. Most of it had a rather odd taste that I could really do without and the English toothpaste had a rather medicinal taste.

Mom and dad were tireless in their effort to keep me in American supplies and the only interruptions were caused by shipping delays, not because mom and dad had missed sending my care packages out on time.

I was always happy to get the notice to pick up a package from the Bell Helicopter mail room because I never knew what surprises would be waiting for me inside. Mom would always send me pictures, books, cookies and anything else she thought I might enjoy. She always wanted to send me candy but I told her it could only be candy that was not affected by heat, so the candy I got was always hard sugar candy. One time she sent me a plastic jar of Canadian maple syrup for my pancakes that I occasionally made for breakfast.

That was such a delightful surprise, I think I finished off the whole jar in two weeks.

Ten Months in Iran
Assassin's Castle

Sohila and I saw more and more of each other and I became a constant fixture at her sister's house on most weekends. On one such weekend Soraya suggested we go on a picnic to Assassin's castle south of Isfahan. I knew the spot she was talking about because it was marked on my aerial map and I'd flown over it many times. Soraya fixed the picnic basket while Sohila and I sat in the garden kissing and talking. She was concerned about the civil unrest that was taking place in Tehran and that people had been killed by the army. She said the mullahs were upset by the Shah's attempt to modernize Iran. As we talked it was apparent that she couldn't see the dichotomy of the mullah's protest. On the one hand they are telling the Iranians that they are going to modernize the economy and build a better society while on the other hand they protest the Shah's attempt to modernize Iran and expand their economic sphere beyond the borders of the country.

First, what the mullahs were really protesting was that they wanted to be in charge of the new government and second, they wanted to eliminate all Western influences (movie theaters, music, dancing, TV, Western clothing and the freedom not to be hogtied by your religion) that they claimed the Shah imported from the United States. They wanted to make every city in Iran just like Qum[11] where there are no theaters, no TV, no Western music, no dancing and no alcohol.

The power of Iran's mullahs was greatly eroded during the Shah's rule because he purchased land from the mullahs (at the price they claimed the land was worth on their tax forms, even though mullahs are exempt from paying taxes) and redistributed that land to peasants on

---

[11] Qum is the religious center of Iran and is located between Isfahan and Teheran.

long term payment plans. The mullahs got most of the land they owned because it was willed to them by rich men who they assured would be granted a special place in heaven because of their gift. This made the mullahs rich and the families left behind poor and landless. The mullahs would then share crop the land and collect a constant tax free income.

When we arrived at the site of the Assassin's castle, Soraya set up the picnic in the shade of a large rock while Sohila and I climbed up to look at what remained of the castle. Most of the castle was destroyed but the foundation and some of the lower rooms had partially survived. We were about sixty feet up into the ruins and standing in one of the storage rooms when I realized that we were actually alone for the first time. She was talking to me but I couldn't hear what she was saying; my thoughts were somewhere else. I held my hands out to her and she immediately walked into my arms. I closed my eyes as I pulled her close and kissed her. We held the kiss for a long time. He full lips were so soft I felt like I was sinking into her as we kissed. When I finally gave up her mouth I moved her thick hair out of the way and started kissing her on the neck.

The taste of salt from her perspiration and the scent of perfume from her hair accelerated my excitement. I had never particularly cared for sweaty women before but for some reason the taste of her perspiration was causing me to experience an erotic episode. I was not the only one whose heart was pounding and was breathing hard. She was holding onto me just as hard as I was holding onto her. I wanted to feel her breasts so much but I didn't want to be too bold. So I moved my hands up under her arms and then forward just far enough so that the palms of my hands were touching the sides her breasts and kissed her

Ten Months in Iran

again. She responded by putting both of her arms around my neck. I explored both of her breasts while we kissed. Between the body heat and the hot desert sun we were both drenched with sweat when we broke apart. I told her that we should try to dry off a little before we get back down to where Soraya was waiting for us. We found an area between two tall rocks where there was a breeze and cooled down before returning. As we approached Soraya she looked at us and asked if we had had fun up on the mountain. Sohila said something to her in Farsi and they both laughed so I figured everything was ok.

Sohila told me that this was the original location and the birthplace of a group of people who were known as the assassins and that they established a stronghold here in the mountains of Iran in the 12th century. They assassinated important Sunni Muslim religious leaders and political leaders they didn't agree with.

The Assassins were a splinter group from a subgroup of Ismailis, a branch of eleventh century Shiite Muslims. The Ismailis were most important from the 10th to the 12th century emerging from an early dispute (765 AD) over the succession of the sixth imam. The Shia Muslims acknowledged Jafar al-Sadiq as the sixth imam and they recognized Ismail, his eldest son, as his legitimate successor. On Ismail's death however, the Ismailis acknowledged Ismail's son Muhammad as the seventh and last imam, whose return on Judgment Day they await. That is why the Ismailis are known as the Seveners, because they accept only the first 7 imams where Shia Muslims recognize 12 imams.

In the eleventh century this castle would have been impossible to take by force and anyone laying siege to it would have had to isolate it for a year in order to starve them out because they'd built huge cisterns for water, large rooms to hold grain and areas to hold livestock. All the rain that fell on the castle was directed into the cisterns. Sohila couldn't tell me what finally brought them down and I have never able to find a book about them. I enjoyed the outing even though it was hot and almost everything we ate or drank had sand in it.

I found out later the only picnics they ever had were for the celebration of *Sizdar Bidar* at the end of the *Now Ruz,* a Zoroastrian holiday that most Iranians still celebrated. Zoroastrianism, Sohila informed me, was the first state religion of Persia and the world's first monotheistic religion. The Zoroastrian religion, started approximately 600 years before the birth of Christ, has had more influence on the world's subsequent major monotheistic religions (i.e., Judaism, Christianity and Islamism) than any other social order. The ideas of the devil, hell, judgment day, resurrection, a future savior, confession and an afterlife all came from Zoroastrianism.

The Zoroastrians had a concept of "dual forces competing to create a harmonious result" that sounds amazingly like the Chinese concept of yin and yang that existed 400 years before the Zoroastrians. I wonder if some early Zoroastrians traveled to China to get this idea or if the existence of opposites is primordial and thus a universal idea. Also, the three wise men who visited Jesus at his birth were, I have read, Zoroastrians from Persia.

The yearly Iranian Zoroastrian picnic was normally held in city parks with thousands of other picnickers. So Soraya and Sohila had never had a picnic quite like this before and had done it just for me because they had read that it was an American tradition and thought I would enjoy it. They were right. It gave me an entire day to relax and talk with two lovely and intelligent women.

Ten Months in Iran

I had promised Tim that I would go to an Iranian restaurant with him that evening so I had to leave the ladies at five and return home. He liked to try the local Iranian restaurants but didn't like going alone so I occasionally went along to keep him company.

Iranian Restaurant

During my military career I lived and worked in several countries and in each country I ate their food, listened to their music and became comfortable with their customs. The people in most countries I have been in are more or less just like the people in the United States - they work, they play, they have wives and children whom they love and enjoy being with. But, I can't recall any of the countries that I have been in that presented me with as many unique experiences as Iran.

The Iranian restaurant we visited this evening was one of those unique experiences. I was stunned by the lack of ambiance and décor. It was like traveling back in time and going into an early restaurant the Amish might have set up in Ohio 1800. The restaurant occupied a second floor room that was about twenty feet long and fifteen feet wide. The dining area was drab, no coverings on the windows and a bare unpainted wood floor. The tables were made from ruff-cut unfinished wood and were also bare, no placemats or table cloth. The only light came from a single bare light bulb hanging from the ceiling. The term rustic is grossly inadequate when trying to describe the dining room.

There were no women in this restaurant. The cook was male, the waiter was male and all the customers were male and old. When we walked into the room everyone looked at us like we had just arrived from a different planet, and I guess we had.

Ten Months in Iran

The menu was easy, they had kebob, rice, bread and tea, so we ordered everything on the menu. I will have to admit that it was the best kebob and rice that I have ever had, but the bread was stale and the tea was questionable. Tim told me the Iranians invented the kebob and were very proud of it.

The Iranian Psyche

Tim and I weren't back at home long before Mahmoud stopped by to visit. He wanted to ask me about Soraya. He was interested in finding out if she had any other boy friends.

"As far as I know, Mahmoud, she is only seeing you." I said.

"She's ten years older than I am but it doesn't make any difference to me because she's a terrific lady."

"I agree with your assessment about her being a terrific lady; besides, she doesn't look her age anyway." I said.

I told him that he was lucky because the two of them could go almost anyplace and not have to put up with the looks that Sohila and I got. He asked me why I thought people would notice the two us and I told him that I was fifteen years older than Sohila.

"Well," he said, "Soraya isn't the only one who's holding her age well. I had no idea you were that much older than Sohila."

We started talking about the Iranian pilots and airmen that we worked with and how confusing it was sometimes to know what to say or do around them because you never knew what they believed or what they were thinking.

"The more male Iranians I come to know, the more I am convinced that they are all, to some degree, schizophrenic. If you talk to any male Iranian long enough you can easily

Ten Months in Iran

detect serious contradictory and conflicting ideas, attitudes and behaviors." Mahmoud said.

"I know what you mean. " I said. "They hate the United States but want more than anything else to go to the US. They dislike Americans but when you go to their homes or work with them they treat you like a long lost brother. They love to drink alcohol but think it should be banned from their society. They love to see Western movies and even have a black market in them, but think it is right to ban them from their society. At times I felt like that computer in the *Star Trek* episode where Captain Kirk caused it to meltdown by repeatedly feeding it illogical information."

"What's amazing to me," Mahmoud said, "is that they don't see anything illogical or inconsistent in the way they feel or think. The few Iranians with whom I felt comfortable enough with to talk about Islam further convinced me of their schizophrenia. We talk about women's rights and they tell me that men and women are equal but different."

"Well," I said, "The black people in the states know what that phrase means, don't they?"

"Yes, we do, and then I'm told that men and women have different rights and responsibilities and that their roles are determined by society. When I asked who 'society' is they tell me Islam. I asked why a woman's testimony in court is only worth half as much as a man's testimony. They say they aren't familiar with that law. I also asked why, between a brother and sister, the man gets twice as much property as the woman when an estate is settled. They say they aren't familiar with that law either. Then I suggested to them that only mullahs, who're all men, interpreted the Qur'an and thus determined the rights that would be granted to women. I got an agreement on this point and then they said that it was right to be that way and that the mullahs were dedicated to protecting Islamic women. At this point I gave up the idea of convincing them that women really didn't have any rights that might possibly conflict with what men thought constituted a perfect male society."

Role Model for Christina

I talked to Christina's mother about her acting more like a boy than a young lady and she told me that she was aware of her daughter's shortcomings. I also asked her what she thought about my taking Christina out with Sohila so she could see how a lady is supposed to conduct herself in a restaurant and nightclub. She tried to make excuses for the way Bob had raised her and that they never had any money to take her out to fine restaurants. When I found out that Christina had just had a birthday, I gave her mother some money to buy her a party dress and told her that I would be there to pick her up at six o'clock on Friday for supper at the Kourosh and that I would have her home by ten o'clock. She told me she would have her ready at six.

I told Sohila and Soraya about Christina needing a role model and asked if they would try to coach her. They were actually a little excited about meeting her because they had never met an American teenager. I told them that she was a little crude, but I didn't tell them about her gassing me on the couch. They told me that they would meet Christina and me in the lobby of the Kourosh at six thirty on Friday.

When I pulled up in front of Christina's apartment I saw her at the window awaiting my arrival. He mother met me at the door and told me that Christina was excited about having a night out. She also told me that she had worked with her that day in an effort to 'smooth out some of her rough edges' as she put it. Christina had on a new party

Ten Months in Iran

dress that definitely accentuated her feminine side. I had always thought she was a little overweight because she always wore big floppy shirts and pants. Seeing her in a dress, I realized that she had a terrific shape and large breasts.

As I had planned, Christina and I arrived at the Kourosh hotel a few minutes before Soraya and Sohila and waited for them in the lobby. Christina was the main attraction in the lobby; every man who walked through the lobby looked at her for as long as possible. She was totally unaware of the attention she was getting so I pointed it out to her. I thought it would be a good ego boost for her and I also thought it would get her to feel more like a woman. All I managed to do was to make her feel self conscious about the way she looked and she started slouching in an effort to hide her breasts. Then I got a feeling of déjà vu as I gave her the same lecture that I had given to my own daughters when they first became aware of their breasts and the fact that men liked to look at them.

When Soraya and Sohila walked into the lobby they looked more beautiful than I could have ever imagined. They both had on black gowns I hadn't seen before Soraya's was trimmed in gold and Sohila's was trimmed in white lace. Their hair was pushed up high in a way that I hadn't seen before either. Sohila, who was normally four inches shorter than I, was now an inch or so taller because of her high heels and hair. When I introduced Christina to them I noticed she wasn't slouching anymore. I was worried that they may not have anything to talk about considering their age and education differences, but the only thing I wound up having to worry about was how to get a word in myself. There were a few times during the evening when I think I could have gone home and no one would have noticed. I finally got Soraya away when the band started to play and I asked her to dance. She thought Christina was a lovely young girl and didn't see where there was any problem. I got the same report from Sohila when I danced with her. She thought Christina was beautiful and interesting and wanted me to bring her over to the house some weekend so they could get better acquainted.

Christina didn't want to dance at first but I talked her into it and, once on the floor and hidden in the crowd, she did quite well. She said her mother had spent some time with her that day teaching her to dance. She thanked me while we were dancing and told me that she was having a wonderful time. She said she liked Soraya and Sohila and would like to see them again. I had the last dance with Sohila just before we left the club and told her that I thought she was stunningly beautiful and that I would remember what she looked like in that gown for as long as I lived. She told me that she hoped I would live for at least a hundred years.

I walked Christina to her door but didn't go in because I knew her mother was waiting to hear all about her evening out and I didn't want to infringe on their newly discovered mother-daughter relationship.

The Sandstorm

Isfahan in the summer is mostly hot, dry and sunny. There were weeks at a time when there wasn't a single cloud, and the temperature would vary between 110^0 and 120^0F. On the hottest days we couldn't fly because the aircraft was too hot to touch even while wearing flight gloves. One hot day while performing a pre-flight inspection with my crew chief I suddenly felt a cool breeze. I was wondering where a cool breeze could be coming from and

Ten Months in Iran

turned to look at my crew chief. He looked like he had just seen a ghost. "Sandstorm!" he screamed at me. I turned to look in the direction he was pointing and saw a huge brown cloud envelope the mountain that was just three miles west of the airbase. It was like a wall of sand soaring from the ground to five or six thousand feet and coming at us at an incredible rate of speed. My crew chief was franticly trying to get all the inspection doors of the helicopter closed up. I joined him in the effort.

When the wind and sand hit, all I could do was keep my eyes closed and hold on to the helicopter. The wind was so violent that it shook the helicopter. I hid my face but my ears and head felt like they were inside a sand blaster; I didn't have a hat on. That was my first sand storm and I found out that it sometimes rains inside a sandstorm and that a storm can be gone just as quickly as it arrived. When I opened my eyes I was amazed at what I saw. Everything was covered with a thick sandy mud. The Cobra had to be washed before I could fly it and the crew chief and I had to have a shower and a change of clothes. I saw several more sand storms while I was in Iran, some while flying and you don't fly in sand storms if you can keep from it. During one I sat the aircraft down on a remote highway and waited for the storm to pass. On another occasion I saw the storm coming and just flew out of its way.

Flying in Iran took special training when it came to setting down at any of the remote training airfields in the desert, especially if they hadn't been use in awhile. The desert Southeast of Isfahan has very little sand, most of it is a fine talcum powder like dust that envelopes the helicopter every time you land. I used the same approach method the Navy helicopter pilots learned when flying in Antarctica, you pick out a spot on the ground and fly the helicopter into it. You don't come to a hover and feel for the ground. You know when you are going in that you will not see the ground for the last four to five seconds, because of the snow in the Antarctica and the dust in the desert.

The desert, on morning flights before the wind picked up, always had wild dog tracks going in every direction. I asked one of the Iranians about the tracks and he told me that you didn't want to be in the desert at night without some type of protection because the dogs were wild and would attack you if they thought they had a chance to kill and eat you. I had gone through desert survival school in the military and had been advised of the different hazards that the desert presented during the day and the night, but dogs were never on the danger list. After that bit of information I was happy that all my test flights were during the daytime; but I did start to carry my survival knife with me whenever I flew over the desert.

Iranian Airmen

It was impossible not to like the Iranian airmen that I worked with and taught. They were typical young men who wanted to succeed at what they were doing and were eager to learn. They were all interested in, and had a thousand questions about, what life in the United States was like. They also pestered me endlessly for stories about combat in Vietnam. I liked to talk about both subjects, so when I saw them drifting off on hot slow days, I would bring them back with an interesting combat story or tell them about how some everyday things are so different in the United States. One of the things they were so amazed about was the fact that you could go shopping at 2am in most big cities in the states. This subject came up because they were complaining abut not being able to buy anything except on the weekends because they came

Ten Months in Iran

to work in the dark and went home after everything was closed.

The young airmen were also interested in learning American slang and were constantly asking me the meaning of word or slang phrases they had heard on tapes or American TV shows. Iran TV would occasionally show an American TV show and they could also pick up American TV shows from a Turkish station. I had no idea what many of the phrases I was asked about actually meant and would tell them that I would find out and tell them during the next class. They responded well to drawings during my presentations and since I have always been a good artist, I used visual aids that I generated before class. Whenever possible I drew pictures on the chalk board for them. Since they were limited to an eight hundred word vocabulary, I came to appreciate the significance of the old Chinese saying that 'a picture is worth a thousand words'.

Hot and Sunny

You wouldn't think that you could get tired of sunshine, but you can. That summer in Isfahan we had a forty-three day period of time when the weather reports were: hot (105^0 F) and sunny, hot (120^0 F) and sunny, hot (115^0 F) and sunny. I would take off in a helicopter and go looking for a cloud. I never found one during all 43 days. I always knew that a person could become depressed when subjected to weeks of cloudy skies and rain. I had experienced that reaction to the weather in Tennessee when I was a young airman going through the Navy's Electronics Training "A" School in Millington.
Sunshine, after awhile, will induce the same type of depression. On the day that a cloud finally did make an appearance, all the Americans went outside to look at it

127

stealing, because they said they knew he was stealing something.

"Yes," he said, "I was stealing something … wheelbarrows".

Amelda

One Friday evening Jay and Mai came to my house and asked if one of the nurses could spend the next few nights at my place. They explained that Amelda had offended one of the male Iranian orderlies at the hospital and when he became irate with her she gave it right back to him and he threatened to kill her. She was drawing blood from a patient when the orderly came into the room and told her to go clean up a mess in the next room. She told him to do it himself because she was busy and then reminded him that it was his job anyway.

Mai told me that they were treated like slaves at the hospital and even though they were qualified registered nurses they had to do jobs that would normally be done by orderlies. She said if any patient defecated or vomited in their bed, they would be called to clean it up instead of an orderly. She said the Iranian nurses never cleaned anything up. She said Amelda could be fired from her job due to the confrontation because it wasn't long before the doctors and nurses on the floor were all getting in on the action. They told her not to come back until they called her. Now she is afraid that the orderly will try to kill her or do something to her. She is also afraid that she will lose her job and be forced to go back home and lose the bonus we get for completing our contract.

I asked her why they put up with such poor treatment and she told me they did it for the money. She said they made ten times more money working in Iran than they would in the Philippines, if they could even get a job in the Philippines.

Ten Months in Iran

I asked them where Amelda was and they told me she was waiting in the car. I told them she could stay for the night but would have to find someplace else tomorrow night. I told Jay if she stayed with me very long there was a strong possibility that I might kill her. The last time we were together it only took me about three blocks to get tired of her mouth. Mai promised me that Amelda would keep her mouth shut and stay out of my way. After they left, Amelda did exactly what Mai had promised. She slept on the sofa and kept her mouth shut. I stuck a note on Tim's door telling him that we had a temporary house guest.

The next morning she fixed our breakfast and we sat down together at the table and actually had a rational conversation. She was so docile and amenable that I started to feel sorry for her. It was Saturday so I asked her if she wanted to go with me to pick up Christina; I explained that I had her clean my house on Saturday so she could earn some extra money.

During the drive to pick up Christina, Amelda didn't complain about the traffic, the road or the route that I took. I was amazed. It was like this girl had had a brain transplant. Christina and Amelda got along well together and both cleaned my house while I sat on the porch and drank coffee. They not only cleaned, they did my laundry and washed the glass doors, something I didn't normally require of Christina. I paid Christina and rewarded Amelda for her work by taking her with us to lunch at the Korean restaurant. I couldn't get over the change in Amelda. I had been with her all day and she hadn't complained about anything.

I was also very pleased about Christina. I noticed she was wearing more feminine looking clothing when we picked her up and the clothing she was wearing was clean and pressed. I was hoping I would witness some degree of

Ten Months in Iran

transformation in her from a crude teenager into a well behaved young lady and it looked like the desired change was taking place. She also demonstrated improved behavior at the restaurant where she sat down quietly and ate like a lady. As I watched her eat I thought that helping her during her transition from tomboy to womanhood would probably be my most significant achievement in Iran.

Jay and Mai came back that evening and told me that they hadn't been able to find a place for Amelda to stay and asked if she could stay another night. I agreed. That evening she and I sat on the roof, drank Coke and she told me her life story. After listening to her stories I could see why she had such an antagonistic attitude. If I had gone through all the hardships and disappointments that she'd gone through, I would be such a bitch that King Kong would look like Tinker Bell in comparison. She had graduated from medical school as a registered nurse but was never treated like an RN. Her first job was in India and her manager at the hospital thought she was not only a nurse but his personal sex slave. She didn't last long there. Her next job was in Singapore where her manager at the hospital expected her to take care of his children at night after she got off work as a condition for keeping her job at the hospital. She didn't last long there either.

She explained to me what it was like working for Iranians and it reminded me of stories I had read about the treatment of black servants in the United States years ago. She said there were no conversations at work, only commands, and when they went to eat in the lunch room the Iranians wouldn't sit with them or talk to them. The Filipino nurses mostly did jobs that the Iranians didn't want to do because it was either too dirty or considered beneath their status.

Ten Months in Iran

On Sunday Amelda and I were out driving and saw the nomads camped in the city park. They came into Isfahan to shop and trade items they produced during their journey in the desert. The nomads were interesting people - their women wore colorful tribal costumes, went unveiled and wore gold and silver coins sewn to their clothing. A friend told me that some nomads use their wives as a place to keep their money, sort of like a bank that traveled with you. This was mainly due to the fact that they didn't trust city people or the honesty of their banks. Most of the inhabitants of Isfahan tolerated the occasional invasion of their parks by the nomads and the merchants were happy because the nomads were cash customers.

The government had a continuing program to try and get the nomads to settle down somewhere but had little success. They were tribal and had little to do with the government. Their loyalty was to their tribe, although many demonstrated loyalty to the Shah during some of the demonstrations in Isfahan. During one instance, a mob of Shiites was conducting a rather violent demonstration when they came into contact with a group of nomads as they passed a park where the nomads were camped. A major fight erupted and some swords came out resulting in several of the demonstrators being taken to the hospital with severe cuts.

Iran also has bands of gypsies who also come into the city to trade and buy supplies. The gypsies don't enjoy the same cordiality and tolerance afforded the nomads. Somehow they are considered less honorable than the nomads and frequently get into trouble with the police. I often wondered if the trouble was due to the conduct of the gypsies or to the attitude of the police.

Ten Months in Iran

Sunday evening Jay and Mai returned with some good news and to take Amelda back to her apartment. They told us that a higher level official in the hospital used some judgment and squashed the problem before it got too far out of hand and she was to be back at work on Monday.

Required Prayer

Trying to do anything with the Iranians was always a problem. You couldn't predict the length of time it would take to complete a project just because you knew how long it normally took to do the job. If that sounds like a conundrum, it's not. There are different things in Iran that you have to take into consideration.

One big problem with doing anything in Iran is the requirement that they perform four formal prayers to Allah every day, and to pray to Allah they must be clean. So they have to put on a clean shirt, wash their hands and face, then kneel on a prayer rug facing Mecca. The prayer must not be too short or they could be looked upon as not sincere. They can't make love to a woman or touch a pregnant woman and then pray to Allah; so, they must schedule their love life to insure that enough time has passed to enable them to perform their prayers with a clean body (not soiled by touching a pregnant woman).

They pray just before sunup and just after sundown, so you can see the problem. According to how long the daylight lasts they could be praying every two and one half-hours in the winter-time. Considering the time it takes them to get ready and the time necessary for the prayer, they can only work in two-hour increments throughout the day. But wait, they don't work from 2:30 to 4pm because that's a recognized traditional rest period in Iran that was started because it's too hot to work during that part of the day. At least the Iranians don't pray five times a day like they do in Saudi Arabia. I have never seen or heard of any other religion that hogties its believers the way Islam does.

The New House

As I was leaving my house one morning I noticed a horse-drawn wagon across the street unloading what looked like a very large load of manure. That evening when I returned home I could tell that it was indeed manure. During the day someone also had delivered a load of straw and a load of soil. The next morning another wagon was unloading what looked like one-foot square boxes that were about six inches deep. The boxes had no tops or bottoms.
That evening when I returned home I saw an old man and a young boy working in the lot. The old man was shoveling the straw, soil and manure into a flat wooden box that was about five foot square and one foot deep. The boy was adding water and mixing the ingredients with a small shovel and his bare feet. After each batch the old man would scoop up shovels full of the mixture and fill the small boxes that were spread around the lot. After watching them for awhile I decided that they were making building blocks.

The blocks baked in the hot Iranian sun for about a week before the next crew showed up to start building the house. Each day wagons came with loads of straw, soil and manure to be mixed by the old man and the boy and used to make more blocks and as the mortar to bind the cured blocks that were being positioned to form the walls. After a wall was completed a mixture of this straw, soil and manure mortar was applied by hand to each side to give the wall a smooth finish. When all the walls were completed, timbers arrived to make the flat roof. I was anxious to see how they were going to close up the gaps between the timbers when the beams were in place.

Ten Months in Iran

I asked my neighbor about the construction and he told me that it was normal and that the house I was living in was made the same way. To my surprise, after a few weeks they started to put a second floor on the house. As far as I could tell there was nothing connecting the second floor to the first floor, it was like a layer cake. I never got to see how they closed up the gaps between the roof timbers. It took about two and a half months to complete the house and my neighbor was right, after it was completed it looked just like our house except it had two floors. I wouldn't want to be in that house during an earthquake because I'm sure the second floor would collapse into the first floor and kill anyone who was there.

Christina's Visit

I called Soraya Friday night and asked if it would be ok for me to bring Christina to her house for a visit the next day. Soraya said that she would be happy to see Christina again and that she would call Sohila to be sure that she would also be there. After Christina and I finished cleaning my house I took her over to Soraya's.

This was the day that I finally met Reza, Soraya's youngest son. He was tall like his mother, about five ten and 180 pounds. He was an extremely bright boy and we got along really well. I thought he would never shut up; he asked me one question after another for a full hour. He wanted to know everything about the United States and about me and about flying helicopters. I answered all the questions I could but I had to tell him that I hadn't been in all fifty states. I then confessed to him that I had seen more of the world than I had of my own country. He couldn't believe that I had never seen the Statue of Liberty or the Grand Canyon. He asked me about being in combat in Vietnam and told me that he wanted to be a

Ten Months in Iran

soldier and a pilot; however, his mother had different ideas about what he would be, she wanted him to be a doctor and was already talking to medical schools that would take him.

When Reza found out that I collected coins we had another common interest and something more to talk about. He also collected coins so we talked about his coin collection while Soraya and Christina went into the women's side of the house to talk. When Sohila came in, she kissed me on the cheek and walked into the back of the house and I didn't see her again. After about half an hour I asked Reza if he would like to go to the bazaar and see if we could find anything interesting. He said that he would, so I asked him to go into the back and tell the ladies that we were going away for an hour or two.

At the bazaar Reza asked me what I wanted to see and I told him that I also liked antique guns and knives. He took me to a section of the bazaar that I hadn't seen before - the shop was off the main walkway through the bazaar and stuck back in a corner behind another shop. It was full of guns, swords and knives. I was almost afraid to go in, thinking that it must be illegal. However, after my eyes had acclimated to the low light level, I could see that none of the weapons in the shop had been made within the past fifty years. The majority of the weapons were of Arab origin; what I liked to call camel rifles that were probably manufactured somewhere in the desert. Most of the knives and swords were also of Arab origin and were made in the same desert. However, I did find some interesting guns and knives that I would liked to have purchased but thought it would be better not to. I didn't want to have any trouble with the government trying to get them out of the country.

Ten Months in Iran

The interesting items that I found were a 1920 Japanese 8mm Nambu semi-automatic pistol with teak grips, an 1895 Russian 7.62mm Nagant revolver, an English Webley 11mm pistol, a 60cal. English flintlock pistol with a brass barrel and LONDON stamped on the barrel; and a load of Caucasian flintlock pistols that looked like they were about 32 caliber. They had a handful of British Brown Bess flintlock rifles and a couple of Remington Rolling Block rifles that looked like they were probably chambered for a 44-100 cartridge. But they had Arab characters stamped on the barrel and English numbers on the receiver. The only knives they had that were interesting were a Kukri knife used by the Gurkha mercenaries in WWI and a Sheffield dagger used by the British OSS during WWII.

Reza and I spent almost two hours at the bazaar before starting back to Soraya's house. When we arrived the ladies were having a snack in the living room so Reza and I joined them.

"Did you have a good time at the bazaar?" Sohila said.

"Yes, we did. I saw some beautiful antique weapons that I would like to have."

"What type of weapons?" Sohila said.

"Oh, knives, pistols and rifles," I said.

"That is one area where all men are alike around the world." Soraya said.

"Well," I said. "I don't think you'd get anyone to argue that point with you. Weapons are the toys of men."

"Did you buy anything?" Soraya said.

"No, I thought about it but decided not to because I thought it might cause trouble. What did you ladies do while we were away?" I said.

"We talked about things that only ladies talk about." Sohila said.

Ten Months in Iran

"Ok," I said. "I guess I won't go there. Did you have a good time, Christina?"

"Yes, I did. I wish I could just live here with Soraya and Sohila." she said.

"Well, I think I should be taking you home now; your mother will be wondering where you are. She may think that I've run off with you."

"If she thinks that, it is only because she would be jealous." she said.

"Why would you ever say that?" I said.

"Because she told me that she would like to run away with you."

"Oh! I can't believe you said that about your mother."

"It's true!" she said. "She told me she thinks you're intelligent, sophisticated, well mannered and handsome."

"I think we had better get off that subject." I said.

During the drive home, Christina couldn't stop talking about what a terrific time she'd had during her visit with Soraya and Sohila.

"Do you like the way they fixed my hair?" she said.

"Yes, it looks good."

"They couldn't keep their hands out of my hair; they told me that they'd never seen red hair before. Soraya said she had always wanted blond hair until she saw my red hair, now she wants red hair. I told them that I've always hated my red hair. It's too fine and too hard to do anything with."

"I suspect that's a normal woman feeling the world over, but, I think it is more prevalent in societies where all the women have the same color of hair, like Norway where all the ladies are blond or Iran where all the ladies have black hair."

"Well, I feel a lot better about my hair now than I did before. I didn't think anyone ever thought it was beautiful or desirable until I talked to Soraya and Sohila."

Ten Months in Iran

"Sohila has such beautiful clothes. Did you know that we are almost the same size? The only difference is that she has bigger breasts. I tried on several of her dresses and gowns. Some day I'll have clothes like that."

"Christina, I think once you start dressing and acting like the beautiful young lady that I know you are, men will be throwing themselves at your feet to get your attention."

"Well, I don't know about that." she said.

She was quiet for a few moments and then started up again.

"Did you know they have a section of the house that is just for women, a place where women can do what they want to do without worrying about men seeing them or hearing what they are talking about? I think we should start something like that in the United States." she said.

"You are a little late with that idea." I said. "There is already such a place and it's was called a teenage daughter's bedroom."

"I've never had a bedroom all to myself."

"Your dad told me he couldn't find a three bedroom apartment; that's why you have to share your bedroom with your brother."

"I've always had to share a bedroom with my little brother. I didn't have my own bedroom in Georgia."

"Well," I said, "I'm sorry to hear that. I think every young girl should have a bedroom all to herself, or, if it must be shared, to at least share it with a sister."

I delivered her to her door but I didn't go in because I felt self-conscious after what she had told me about her mother.

Alcohol and Drugs

The major hotels in Iran have alcohol and can legally sell it to Westerners. Some of the big hotels that are run by the government also will sell alcohol to Iranians who are

Ten Months in Iran

prosperous enough to stay at the hotel. Except for the rich, Iranians can't buy alcohol in Iran but they can buy opium, heroin and marijuana in and around the bazaar if they know the right person to approach. Opium is used mostly by older men who have money and the practice is generally overlooked by the government. Marijuana and heroin are the drugs of choice of young Iranians and drug abuse is widespread in major cities, all in a land where any diversion from an Islamic lifestyle is frowned upon and illegal.

The Island of Kish

Many of the activities that are not acceptable in Isfahan or Tehran are tolerated and openly promoted on the sunny island of Kish in the Persian Gulf. The island was developed by the Shah of Iran who built hotels and a casino to lure rich Arabs. Iranians were barred without special authorization (i.e., being rich). The Shah tried to present Kish as a European style getaway for the rich and famous of the Arab world. Kish displays its prosperity in the new air-conditioned Mercedes that deliver visitors to the posh hotels. It's promoted as a place where visitors can have a beer and a good time and no one will notice or care. Kish also had American and European goods that visitors couldn't find in Tehran, Isfahan, Riyadh, Muscat or Abu Dhabi and everything was tax free. There were limits though, to what visitors could buy. In the evenings, live American music can be heard coming from the hotels, cafes and restaurants. There were even places where visitors could dance and hold a woman in their arms or, if they have enough money, could have a woman visit them in their room.

I wonder how the island will fare after an Islamic Republic is established by the Ayatollah Khomeini and

Ten Months in Iran

the omnipotent religious police take charge of public morals and scour Iran for signs of Western influence and decadence.

Repairs at Soraya's house

Soraya knew that my dad had been a builder and, because I spent most of my vacation time working with him (it was the only way I got to spend any time with him), that I claimed to be able to fix anything around the house. So, one Saturday she called to see if I could fix a door that was neither closing nor locking properly. I told her if she had the tools, I could fix the problem.

When I arrived at her house she had every tool she could find laying on a small table by the door I was to fix. As it turned out, all I needed to fix the door was my Buck knife and a screw driver. The hinge screws had worked loose from the door jam and, since the repair had not been performed immediately, the screw holes were stripped out. I used my knife to cut some slivers of wood from an old box she had and drove the slivers into the screw holes. I replaced the screws and that job was completed.

Since that task was over so quickly, she wanted to know if I could look at the light switch in her room. She said it only worked sometimes. She asked me if I wanted to turn the electric off and I told her it wouldn't be necessary, that I preferred working with the power on. I pulled the switch and found out that once again she was having a loose screw problem. The ground wire was only occasionally making contact as she wiggled the light switch. She was lucky it hadn't started a fire in the wall. I tightened the screw holding the ground wire.

I could see her mind working. I had been there thirty minutes and had fixed two problems for her already.

"Do you have anything else that needs fixing?" I said.

Ten Months in Iran

"Well," she said. "The water used to empty the toilet doesn't work. I have been using a bucket to empty the toilet."

"Do you mean it won't flush?"

"Yes, it won't flush."

She took me to the WC in the back of the house and pointed to the water tank positioned two meters above the Eastern style toilet.

"Do you have something I can stand on so I can see what's going on up there?"

"Yes, I have a small ladder in the storage room."

She was back moments later with a small ladder. I climbed up, looked into the tank and found another simple problem. The chain that connected the rubber stopper to the release lever had come loose. The tank was full of water, she just couldn't release it. I reached down into the tank, got the chain and reconnected it to the release lever. I got down and pulled the release lever and the toilet flushed.

"I can't believe this." she said. "You've been here less than an hour and have fixed three problems that have been worrying me for months. It would be nice to have you around all the time."

"What else do you have that I can help you with?"

"My sewing machine is jammed."

"Go get it and I'll see what I can do."

She delivered her sewing machine to the small table holding all the tools she had managed to gather together. It was truly jammed. The tension on the rotary hook allowed the bobbin to feed too much thread and the whole area looked like an old fishing reel with back-lash. I cleaned out all the thread and adjusted the tension on the rotary hook and then sewed two small pieces of cloth together to show her that it was working. I showed her how to set the tension on the rotary hook and on the needle feed.

Ten Months in Iran

Just as I finished repairing her sewing machine Sohila arrived. Soraya couldn't stop telling her how handy I was to have around the house and insisted in showing her everything I had fixed. She asked me if I was hungry and then said that she was going to fix me something to eat before I could answer. I took Sohila's hand and led her into the living room where we shared a pillow on the floor. She had spent the morning at home tending to her father. She said he was asleep now and would stay asleep for most of the afternoon.

"Did you know I was here?" I said.

"Yes, we were on the phone when you pulled up in your jeep."

"So, did you come over just to see me?"

"I don't know if I should answer that or not." she said.

"Why not?"

"It might give you a big head."

"A big head?" I said. "What does that mean?"

"Isn't that what you say when someone gets over confident?"

"And you don't want me to be too confident?"

"Well," she said. "I don't want you to stop trying."

"Don't worry, honey. I'll never stop trying."

"Soraya is really impressed with your ability to fix things." she said. "How did you ever learn how to do all those things?"

"Well," I said. "I'll give you my dad's answer. Dad always said that he was so good at fixing things because he was always poor and either had to fix it himself or it didn't get fixed. He never had the money to hire someone else to do the work."

"It must be nice, and save you a lot of money, to be able to fix anything that's broken around the house." she said.

"My ex-mother in-law really appreciated my ability to repair things. Her husband and son were carpenters, but

Ten Months in Iran

when she needed something fixed (and I was home) she called me."

"Why didn't her husband or her son fix things for her?" she said.

"Her husband treated her like a slave and her two sons, as much as I witnessed their relationships, treated her with indifference. Her three daughters were the only family members who really took an interest in her welfare and happiness. Actually, the whole male side of that family would make good Muslims because they believe the only purpose of women is for breeding and that they are possessions like a cow or a mare. The only trouble they would have is that Muslims believe that sons should get 2/3 of an inheritance and daughters should get 1/3; where they believe that sons should get 100% of the inheritance and that daughters should get nothing! Why, they ask, would anyone leave a cow an inheritance?"

145

Ten Months in Iran

Chapter 4
Life Line to Reality

One of the things I enjoyed most in Isfahan, other than Sohila and food, was a wonderful book-store she took me to after I asked her about the availability of American books. I think Isfahan had such a good bookstore because it was a university town. I have always loved the smell of a bookstore, there is just something comforting about it. The Isfahan bookstore was unique because it had an American section, a German section, a French section and a Russian section. I would go there on a Saturday and spend hours looking at the American and German books.

One of the books I purchased there that I was particularly fond of was a special collector's edition of the *Rubaiyat of Omar Khayyam* that had superb illustrations. The accompanying text was in Farsi with translations into English, French and German. Omar Khayyam has been one of my favorite poets since I first started to read poetry thirty years ago. He's not well thought of as a poet in Iran due to his subject matter (love, women and wine), his pessimism about life, his skepticism about religion and his expressed doubt in resurrection and life after death. He is however, remembered for his work in the fields of astronomy and mathematics. He wrote a treatise on algebra demonstrating how to solve cubic equations.

Ten Months in Iran

Omar Khayyam's tomb is in the gardens of the *Imamzadeh Mahruq* located a few miles southeast of the city of Meishabur. I wanted to visit his tomb but never got the opportunity.

Reading Poetry

I could understand only a very few words of Farsi but I would sit or lie in Soraya's living room for long periods of time and listen to Sohila read Omar Khayyam's poetry to me in its original language. I would look at the English translation of the poem she was going to read and then lie back and enjoy it in its original form. She was well versed in poetry in English, Italian and Farsi and to listen to her read was like listening to music. She introduced me to other Iranian poets that I had never heard of, poets like Sasdi and his *The Rose Garden* and *The Orchard,* Hafez and his *Collection of Odes,* Sadeq Hedayat and his *The Blind Owl* (although The Blind Owl was a little too Edgar Allan Poeish for me) and Farid od-Din Attar, a Sufi poet whose poems were too hard to understand and evidently hard to read because Sohila seemed to have had a tough time with them. Still, my all time favorite Iranian poet is Omar.

One day, as she was reading to me, I asked her if she could sing and, at first, she acted embarrassed to answer. But I persisted and she told me that she could sing but not as well as the French lady who sang for us at the club. I asked her to sing something for me in Farsi because it had such a beautiful sound to it during her poetry readings. She told me she would sing an old Persian love song for me. She had such a lovely voice and the tune was so melancholy that it almost made me cry, and I didn't even know what she was saying. She got her little tape player out and sang a few more songs to me in French and

Ten Months in Iran

English. I told her if things ever got too tough for her that she could get a job singing for a living. I don't think she saw that as an option that was open to her though, since Iranian culture looked down on performers.

A Shiite Holy Day

Things had been quiet for a few days in Isfahan and the really serious trouble hadn't reached us yet when I got my promotion to senior pilot. To celebrate, I wanted to have a party at the house and asked Soraya to help me. She told me that, due to the demonstrations, a new rule had just been announced and that if anyone wanted to have any type of a gathering they had to get a permit from the central police station. About noon the next day we set out for the central police station to get the permit. Reza was driving my open jeep and Soraya was sitting in the passenger's seat; Sohila and I were sitting in the back. As the jeep turned onto the main street leading to the police station we could see a throng of men in blood stained white T-shirts coming down the street beating them selves. Soraya's comment was: "Oh, shit. I forgot this was a Shiite holy day."

During Shiite Islam's holy days mourning the martyrdom of the Prophet Muhammad's grandson Hussein (martyred in the 7th century) it is customary to beat oneself bloody with some type of whipping device (e.g., chain, wire rope, rope imbedded with glass) that will rip the skin from your body and make you bleed. It is best to wear a white T-shirt during this demonstration of your dedication to Islam because the blood shows up better. The more you bleed the more favorably Allah looks upon you and the more the observing crowd is impressed with your dedication. During this time of purifying yourself it is encouraged to help purify any young woman who is caught watching the

Ten Months in Iran

event without a chador by beating her until she is either dead or unconscious. They would also help purify any young man who might be acting like he didn't understand the solemnity of the event by displaying improper demeanor.

The Shiite Muslims I knew believed that Allah derived great pleasure form these acts of self-purification and also in participating in the purification of someone else, whether or not that other person wanted the help.

Reza looked for an escape route but we were pinned in by other cars. Soraya quickly pulled out her two emergency chadors and handed one to Sohila and one to me. She instructed each of us to cover every part of our body and to look at the floor of the jeep until we were clear of the mob. Thanks to her, we made it through without any trouble. After we were past the demonstration and looked around I could see blood on the jeep and our clothing from the bleeding self-flagellating demonstrators. I was more in fear for my life driving through that mob than I had ever been in Vietnam.

While we were waiting to see someone at the police station Soraya told me to request a police officer to attend the party because that would assure a permit would be issued and that we would not be harassed by anyone during the party. She was the most street-smart lady I ever met in Iran and she, and the banker's wife, were the only two ladies I ever talked to that thought the return of the Ayatollah Khomeini was going to lead to a disaster. It was easy to see why she didn't want the Ayatollah to return to Iran. She had been Westernized, she liked pretty clothes, parties, dancing, drinking and men, all the things the Ayatollah was against. For her, living in Iran under strict Islamic law would be like being sentenced to hell.

Ten Months in Iran

My alcohol-free party was a big success. I invited several of my co-workers and their girl friends or wives and I told Soraya to invite Mahmoud. Sohila told me that her sister and Mahmoud were getting along really well. Bob and Alice were there and Christina introduced them to Soraya and Sohila. It was the first time they had met and they spent a lot of time talking about Christina. There was a lot of music and dancing and not only the single men, but the married men, wanted to dance with Christina. I began to think my party was actually a 'coming out' party for her.

I made sure the police officer, who spoke very good English, had plenty to eat and that he was included as much as possible in the activities. We played a game where the guests were divided into two groups and a member of one group pulls a slip of paper from a jar and then tries to get his or her team to guess the word that is written on the paper in one minute, and they had to do it without talking. For someone working in a foreign language, Sohila demonstrated great skill at this game.

After the party was over I thanked the police officer for coming and gave him an American ten dollar bill for imposing on his free time. He was noticeably pleased by the gesture. Sohila, Soraya and Mahmoud stayed after everyone else had gone. We sat in the living room in the dark listening to Mozart. Soraya and Mahmoud were on the couch and Sohila was sitting on my lap in an overstuffed easy chair. We spent nearly an hour talking and kissing; I wanted so much to feel her bare breasts; but I didn't because it would've been too embarrassing if the lights had suddenly come on.

Ten Months in Iran
The Law, Shiites and Sunnis

Mahmoud and I frequently got together and talked about Islam and how radicals had managed to distort it over the years. He knew how serious I was about Sohila and wanted to let me know about possible problems we could have in a mixed marriage.

"We could have some culture-related problems," I said. "But I don't think we will have religious problems because I don't have a religion in the sense that others do."

"What do you mean by that?"

"I mean that I don't believe in God the way everyone else does."

"You don't believe in God?"

"That's not what I said. I said that I don't believe in God in the same manner as everyone else. First of all, I believe man is too stupid to know anything of God; and I don't think God has as much interest in us as we do of the ants that live under our feet. Think about it. We are talking about a cognizant being capable of placing the universe into motion. Now, think about this. We can see the universe and can't define it, so what makes us think we can define the God, who we can't see, that created it? I maintain that we are too stupid to know anything of God."

"So, how do you think we should regulate our lives if there is no way of knowing God?"

"I think we should follow the teachings of Moses, Jesus and Mohamed who have set down standards for developing and maintaining successful social societies."

"That would never work, Jack."

"I know it wouldn't. People have got to believe someone is watching them before they will be good Christians, Jews or Muslims."

"So how do you conduct your life, Jack?"

Ten Months in Iran

"I follow the Ten Commandments, the Golden Rule and the laws of the country I'm living in."

We then got in to a discussion about how some Muslims got lost in their religion and Mahmoud gave me his theory.

"Characteristically," Mahmoud said, "The Christians study their Bible and the Jews study their Torah for its theological message and content. Both religions glean from their respective books what they consider to be rules for conducting their lives in accordance with what they believe God expects from them. These rules do not replace their system of enacting and obeying civil laws, a system that they inherited from the ancient Romans and have improved over the centuries. The rules they receive and follow from their respective religions enhances the effectiveness of society and the civil law that maintains order in that society."

"That sounds amazingly like what I said we should do."

He agreed with me that, with the exception of the Jews and Christians believing that God is watching them, my idea of maintaining social order is the same as theirs.

"Early Muslims, on the other hand," he said, "had no ancient ties to a society ruled by an established set of civil laws so, when they found themselves in need of a legal system to prop up their political aspirations, they chose the Qur'an as the basis of all laws. So, the Muslims, study the Qur'an not only for its theological message and content to enhance their relationship with God, but to squeeze out the basis of a civil law through interpretation of the Qur'an. They also tried to develop rules of behavior based on the example of the Prophet and on the society that lived in Medina during his lifetime. With this process in mind it is easy to see why Muslims make no distinction between their religion and their law. The Muslim's all encompassing legal system (derived from interpreting the Qur'an) is contained in a document called the *Sharia*.

Ten Months in Iran

They believe that this legal system should govern every aspect of Islamic life and that it should be the basis of life in Iran today. This approach to Islam makes it look like Islam is more concerned about what people do than about what people believe."

"One of my problems with Islam," I said, "is that Muslims will tell you that there are no priests or clergy in Islam, however, they will continue to admit that there are *ulama* who are Qur'an scholars and there are *fuqaha* who are custodians of the *Sharia*. To me, saying there is no priesthood in Islam is like saying there are no priests in the Vatican. I have always liked the old farmer's test: if it looks like a duck, if it sounds like a duck and if it walks like a duck … it must be a duck."

"Well," Mahmoud said, "I'm not sure I can argue with that since I don't know the exact definition of what constitutes a priest. However, I believe that Arab Muslim's preoccupation with the law is posing a danger to Islam because it's leading to the loss and contamination of the theological spirit of Islam. Your religion should be between you and God, not between you and the state."

Shiites and Sunnis

My banker neighbor told me that most "base intellect Shiites", as he referred to them, believe that if you're not a Muslim, you're an infidel and that they don't consider infidels real people and as such can't be sinned against. What that means, he told me, is if a Shiite steals something from an infidel it isn't a crime in the eyes of Allah. And, he added, if a Shiite kills an infidel it may be a crime in the eyes of the civil law but it's not a crime in the eyes of Allah. There are those individuals, he said, who think Allah takes joy in the killing of infidels and that infidels you kill become your slaves in the after life. I asked him what he thought the basic everyday difference was between Iranian Shiite and Sunni Muslims. He told me that he thought the basic everyday difference was that Iranian Sunnis liked to make money and Iranian Shiites liked to make trouble. I couldn't tell if he was serious or being factious with me; but his opinion wasn't foreign or unique.

While living in Iran I became acquainted with both Shiite and Sunni Muslims. Sohila, Soraya and her son, my two neighbors and my landlord were all Sunni. At a friend's party and at work I became friendly with a few Shiites. I came to believe that there is little in common between the two sects of Islam. The Sunnis impressed me as being interested in making a comfortable living and providing for their families. They practiced their religion but didn't particularly care what you did as long as you didn't interfere with them. Most of the Sunnis I came to know were engineers, bankers, intellectuals, shopkeepers and merchants (not bazaaris[12]).

The Shiites, on the other hand, struck me as being militant, antagonistic and wanting to create a world Islamic state where everyone could enjoy being subjected to their interpretation of Islamic laws and customs. During the period of time I was in Isfahan several Sunnis were murdered and their shops looted and burned because they'd refused to go along with Shiite imposed shutdowns and demonstrations against the Shah. Nearly every single act of violence I read about while I was in Iran was committed by a Shiite Muslim and every violent demonstration I witnessed was led by Shiite Muslims.

---

[12] Bazaar merchants who are highly political

Ten Months in Iran
Where the Shiite-Sunni Problem Began

The death of Muhammad in June of 632 AD left the Muslims leaderless. He had no living sons and hadn't left any instructions on who should be the next leader of the Muslim faith. His first wife, Khadija, gave him two sons, Qasim and Abdullah, and four daughters: Zainab, Ruqayyah, Fatima and Umm Kulthum, but his sons died in infancy. Only Fatima survived and produced living children that provide Muhammad's present-day descendants who are either Sharifs or Sayyids. Ali ibn Abi Talib, Fatima's husband, was Muhammad's first cousin. They had two sons, Hasan and Hussein, who were only five or six years old at the time of his death.

Many thought that Ali, Muhammad's cousin, adopted son and son-in-law should be the one to take charge and lead the Muslim faith. Others wanted to select a man of wealth and position, so a wealthy cloth merchant named Abu Bekr was elected. He had been a close friend of the Prophet's and one of the first to believe in the new religion, He was given the title Khalifah rasul Allah, *Successor to the Messenger of God.* Those who wanted Fatima's husband Ali to assume the leadership role were extremely irritated by the selection of Abu Bekr, thus starting a 1350 year difference of opinion within the ranks of Islam.

Twenty four years after the appointment of Abu Bekr, the third Khalifah, Khalifah Othman was assassinated and the title of Khalifah fell to Fatima's husband Ali. His supporters regarded him as the first true Khalifah while others accepted him as the fourth Khalifah. Some Arabs bitterly opposed his appointment, caused him a considerable amount of trouble and finally assassinated him. He was the Khalifah for only five years.

Muawiya, the nephew of Khalifah Othman, fought for and won the office of Khalifah from the sons of Ali, further exacerbating the longstanding dispute over the right to leadership. Shiite Muslims continued to maintain that the leadership of Islam must remain within the family of Muhammad and that Ali and his descendants are the only ones who have the right to lead the Muslim faith.

The majority of Muslims (the Sunni) believe that the Khalifah can be any qualified Muslim; so, the minority Shiites must endure the rule of the Sunni Khalifahs who are not descendants of Muhammad and this is a constant source of trouble between the two groups. Shiites can be found throughout the Muslim world but they are heavily concentrated in Iran. The Iranian mullahs who wear the black turban claim to be descendants of Muhammad's grandchildren Hasan or Hussein.

Ten Months in Iran

Khalifah rasul Allah
Successor to the Messenger of God

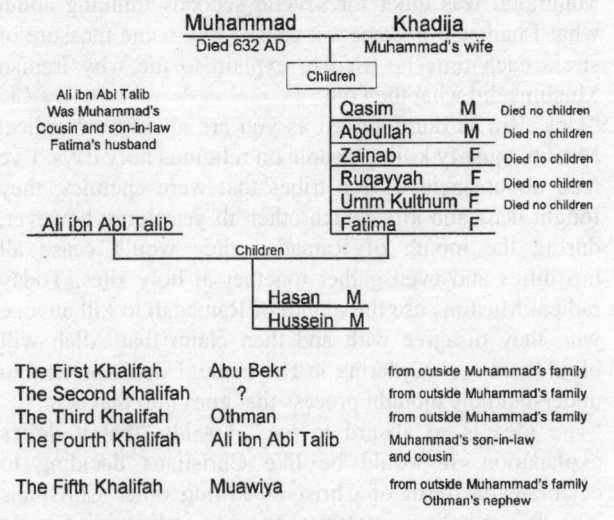

Muhammad	Khadija
Died 632 AD	Muhammad's wife

Ali ibn Abi Talib
Was Muhammad's
Cousin and son-in-law
Fatima's husband

Children:

Qasim	M	Died no children
Abdullah	M	Died no children
Zainab	F	Died no children
Ruqayyah	F	Died no children
Umm Kulthum	F	Died no children
Fatima	F	

Ali ibn Abi Talib

Children:

Hasan	M
Hussein	M

The First Khalifah	Abu Bekr	from outside Muhammad's family
The Second Khalifah	?	from outside Muhammad's family
The Third Khalifah	Othman	from outside Muhammad's family
The Fourth Khalifah	Ali ibn Abi Talib	Muhammad's son-in-law and cousin
The Fifth Khalifah	Muawiya	from outside Muhammad's family Othman's nephew

The Shiites consider Ali ibn Abi the first Khalifah and believe that only the Descendants of Muhammad can be the Khalifah rasul Allah.

Celebrating Religious Holidays

Mahmoud and I were sitting on my front porch talking about the trouble in Iran one day after a Shiite holiday celebration had taken the lives of ten Sunni Muslims.

"One idea that escapes me" I said, "more than any other Islamic practice I have observed in those who profess to be devout Muslims is that of celebrating a holy religious holiday by killing other people. The Qur'an says that Allah created the first man and the first woman and that he created them equal. Therefore, we must all be descendants of that man and woman and that makes all of us distant relatives and creations (children) of Allah. What would lead a Muslim to think that the Father would enjoy

Ten Months in Iran

and even reward one of His children for killing another of His children during a holiday set aside to worship Him?"

Mahmoud was quiet for several seconds thinking about what I had said. I suspect it caused him some measure of stress each time he tried to explain to me why Iranian Muslims did what they did.

"Jack, I'm as dumfounded as you are about how radical Muslims justify killing people on religious holy days. I've read about ancient Arab tribes that were enemies; they fought wars and killed each other all year long; however, during the month of Ramadan they would cease all hostilities and even gather together at holy sites. Today radical Muslims use the month of Ramadan to kill anyone who they disagree with and then claim that Allah will bless them for murdering in His name. I don't pretend to understand the thought process that goes into that act."

"The idea is so absurd to me," I said, "that it defies explanation. It would be like Christians deciding to celebrate the birth of Christ by killing other Christians who do not believe exactly as they do and deciding to do it on Christmas day. Yet, year after year Muslims chose to celebrate their most holy Islamic holidays by killing other Muslims (usually Shiites killing Sunnis), Jews or Christians."

"Jack," Mahmoud said. "I have the feeling that radical Muslim clerics have hijacked Islam and are using it as a tool to promote their own agenda; there is no other explanation. I think their exploitation of Islam is made possible because most Middle East Muslims do not understand the Qur'an. They memorize verses from the Qur'an like school children memorize poems, but, like you have said, memorizing something doesn't mean you understand the concept."

Ten Months in Iran
People of the Book

"Jack, true Muslims who follow the teachings of the Qur'an don't hate Jews or Christians and, in fact, are told by the Qur'an to respect them for their belief in a monotheistic religion and belief in the Last Day and the prophets Moses and Jesus. The Qur'an calls the Jews and Christians *the People of the Book* or *the People of the Scripture* according to which translation you have."

He got his copy[13] of the Qur'an and pointed out two places to me where these ideas are presented.

Qur'an: Chapter (Surah) II "The Cow"

62. Lo! those who believe (in that which is revealed unto thee, Muhammad), and those who are Jews, and Christians, and Sabaeans - whoever believeth in Allah and the Last Day and doeth right - surely their reward is with their Lord, and there shall no fear come upon them neither shall they grieve.

"The line '*They are not all alike*' is meant to differentiate between people who are religious and people who just pretend to be religious."

Qur'an: Chapter (Surah) III "The Family of Imran"

113. They are not all alike. Of the People of the Scripture there is a staunch community who recite the revelations of Allah in the night season, falling prostrate (before Him).
114. They believe in Allah and the Last Day, and enjoin right conduct and forbid indecency, and vie one with another in good works. These are of the righteous.

---

[13] The translation used here is from original Arabic by Marmaduke Pickthall and published by Alfred A. Knopf in 1930.

Ten Months in Iran

115. And whatever good they do, they will not be denied the meed (reward) thereof. Allah is Aware of those who ward off (evil).

Supper at the Palace

After finishing lunch at Soraya's house one Saturday I asked if she could think of someplace different to eat supper, someplace we hadn't tried yet. She told me about a palace that had belonged to the Shah when he lived in Isfahan. She said that it had been converted into a hotel and restaurant and that it was the most beautiful place she had ever seen. I asked her to call and make reservations for the three of us for that evening. She said she would make the arrangements and suggested that Sohila and I go sit in one of the rooms in a section of the house that I knew was normally reserved for women. I thought she may have done this to keep Reza from walking in on the two of us holding each other and kissing. The room had a beautiful thick Persian run scattered with big soft pillows. This was a dangerous situation, we were lying down together, almost concealed in the big pillows, hugging and kissing and she had on a loose blouse, a short skirt, no shoes and bare legs. This was a level of temptation that was reaching a critical point and my erection was at a critical point also, I couldn't hide it.

I laid back and suggested that we rest for awhile because my emotions were getting out of control. She giggled as she rested on the pillow. She actually giggled; I had never heard her make a sound like that before. I wondered if she was purposely tormenting me knowing that I couldn't do anything because her sister could walk in at any time. I waited until my erection went down and then asked to wash my hands. When I returned we sat with our backs against the wall and talked until Soraya came to get us.

Ten Months in Iran

Soraya was right; it was the most opulent structure I had ever seen, it made the Kourosh hotel look like a dog house. What surprised me was the fact that we were allowed to wonder around the converted palace and look at everything. Soraya talked to one of the maids working in the hotel and got her to show us one of the rooms. The room did not comply with the standard Iranian apartment. We walked in on a beautiful blue marble floor entry way that led to a sitting room that had, what appeared to me to be, sixteenth century French gold-colored furniture arranged around a very large Persian rug. There were European oil paintings on the walls and royal blue drapes trimmed in white lace on the windows. The bedroom also had gold colored French style furniture arranged around another large Persian rug. The bathroom was definitely not Iranian; it was a Western style bathroom but had an old style European commode[14]. All the hardware in the bathroom appeared to be gold plated. All the rooms and the restaurant opened onto the courtyard.

The courtyard was a garden that took up about two acres of land. It had fountains, pools (not for swimming), waterfalls and footpaths equipped with convenient comfortable chairs and sofas where you could sit and enjoy the garden and the sound of the water.

The food in the restaurant was a match for the opulence of the building. They had a French chef who did what only the French can do with food. We had cherries jubilee for desert and I thought Sohila was going to jump out of her chair, she got so excited. She said she had never seen anything like that before. After we finished eating we took our drinks into the garden and sat and talked for nearly an hour. During that hour Soraya said she wanted to explore

---

[14] American commodes have the flushing hole in the back; European commodes have the flushing hole in the front.

Ten Months in Iran

more of the palace, but I think she did it just to give Sohila and me some time alone.

"Would you ever consider leaving Iran to live someplace else? I said.
"I have thought about living in some other country where I could do something with my education." she said.
"What would you like to do?"
"I would like to be a teacher of languages."
"What countries would you consider living in?"
She didn't hesitate one moment to give me an answer to that question.
"There are several countries I would consider living in, the United States, England, Italy or France."
"Did you list those countries in their order of precedence?"
"Of course I did."
I had been waiting to ask her another question for a long time and I thought this was as good a time as any. She had told me that she liked me as soon as she saw me at the party when we first met; what I wanted to know was what she saw in me that cause her to be attracted to me.
"You looked like you would be very gentle and I thought you looked soft and cuddly.
"Soft and cuddly,' I said, "I have been called a lot of things in my life, but soft and cuddly was never on the list."
"I was right too, in my feelings about you; because you are gentle, soft and cuddly. You also smell good and you treat Soraya and me like we are real people whose conversation and ideas are worth listening to. Most Iranian men think smelling bad is a virtue and treating women poorly supports their illusion of superiority."
Well, I thought, now I know why she's twenty-five and not married. I think she is a little too liberated for Iranian culture.

Ten Months in Iran

"Are you two ready to go home?" Soraya said, as she walked up to us.

"I think we're ready." I said. "I would like to thank you for showing me this place, Soraya; I really had a good time and the food was incredible."

"You're welcome, Jack," she said, "and thank you for a lovely evening."

When we returned to Soraya's they heard some bad news on the radio. A group of Islamic Shiite radicals had burned down a theater in Abadan[15] (after barring the exit doors) killing 377 fellow Iranian Muslims. The victims were mostly young adults and children. The problem, and the premise of the attack, was that the Abadan Theater had a reputation of showing Western films. Sohila was so devastated by this news that she couldn't stop talking about it and trying to figure out how anyone could do such a horrible thing. As I looked at her I knew I could tell her the answer but it wouldn't do her any good to know and besides, she wouldn't believe me anyway.

The next day the Shah imposed martial law and a curfew.

Visa for Sohila

I went to the United States Information Agency office in Isfahan to see how much of a problem it would be to get Sohila a visa for the United States and to see what problems we would run into if we tried to get married. I had met the cultural attaché a few weeks earlier in the Kourosh hotel so when I saw him standing in the USIA lobby I took advantage of the chance meeting and asked him about the visa and getting married. He told me the visa would be easy and would only take a couple of

---

[15] Abadan - a Southern Iranian city on the Iraq border and a Shiite Muslims stronghold.

Ten Months in Iran

weeks; however, he advised against getting married in Iran. He said our best bet would be to have Sohila go to the states on a visitor's visa and then get married there. He also told me the fewer people who knew of our plans to get married the better off we would be. I thanked him for his answers and for his advice.

Ten Months in Iran

Chapter 5
Enemies Lining Up
Trouble with Russia

One day in October, while at work, I noticed a sense of urgency and agitation among the Iranian pilots that I hadn't seen before. I asked one of the pilots what was going on and he told me they were conducting military exercises near the Caspian Sea around Gorgan when one of the Chinooks either crossed over the border into the Soviet Union or just got too close to the border because the Russians shot it down. Then, when they sent another Chinook to check on the distress signal the first aircraft had transmitted, it too was shot down. He said that the entire military force of Iran had been put on alert and that they were sending ground troops to the area to retrieve the bodies and determine if the aircraft had been over the border.

Over the next few days the activity around the air base was heavy; aircraft were arriving and departing at a wartime pace. It wasn't long before I saw aircraft in the hangar being repaired that had bullet holes in them. I knew that something serious was taking place somewhere. One of the Iranian pilots told me that Russia and Iran had been arguing and fighting over the division of the Caspian Sea and the location of the border in that area ever since oil was discovered there. He said they signed a treaty in

Ten Months in Iran

1940 but it hadn't stopped the bickering over the location of the border, and he expected the disagreement to continue for the next fifty years. As far as I could determine, the only casualties in the dispute were the two Chinook crews and passengers they may have been transporting. There was little mention of the action in the local papers. After a few weeks things settled down and returned to normal.

Trouble with Afghanistan

In November the entire event took place again. This time I was told they were having trouble with infiltrators on the Afghanistan border. I learned that the Afghani invaders were not only coming across the border but were setting up camps inside Iran. Again we went through the frantic arrival and departure of aircraft and once again I saw aircraft being repaired that were full of bullet holes. One of the pilots said that a Cobra had been shot down on the Afghanistan border by a ground-to-air missile. The Iranians were setting up a forward operating base closer to the border so I knew that this battle was not going to be as short lived as their border dispute with the Russians.

The battle went on for weeks and I started to lose students from my classes. I was told that they were being assigned to other duties. I thought that the Shah's resources were being spread out across the country too thinly. At this point even I knew that he had troops deployed in Tehran, Isfahan, Bandar-e-Abbas, the border with Russia and now the border with Afghanistan. He was being attacked from all sides and from the inside. This was the point where a few strong words from the United States in support of the Shah and as a warning to his enemies would have prevented the tragedy of the revolution. However, President Carter was so high up on his moral horse that he couldn't see what was going on down at ground level.

Ten Months in Iran
Inside Enemies

The Shah may have tried to play it too safe, but he had some formidable enemies. The Shah was convinced that his old external enemy (Russia) was trying to surround him; and, while he was paying too much attention to them, an old internal enemy (the mullahs) and a new internal enemy (the bazaaris[16]) were joining forces. The mullahs and the bazaaris wanted the Shah out of Iran and they wanted it for essentially the same reason - the Shah was eroding their income base. The mullahs were losing money due to the Shah's land reform policy (i.e., taking millions of acres of land from them and returning it to the people) and the bazaaris were losing money due to the Shah's foreign trade agreements (throughout Iran's history nearly all import and export business, was handled by a consortium of bazaaris). The Shah had made himself two formidable enemies who convinced the people that what he did either did not provide enough help from the government or that his actions were unwarranted interference by the government.

The United States government was telling him to be lenient, and his opponents saw leniencies as a weakness, making them bolder in their attacks and demonstrations. In thirty seven years the Shah took the country from a per capita daily income of .45 cents to a per capita daily income of $6.30 and his enemies complain about the lack of economic improvement. In that same time period he raised the literacy rate from 5% to 50% and established 200 colleges and universities, and they complain about the lack of an education system.

---

[16] Bazaaris – the merchants who ran the Teheran bazaar.

Ten Months in Iran
An Escape Plan

When the demonstrations became more and more violent and directed towards foreigners, Mahmoud and I, along with two other pilots who had their families with them, decided to devise an escape plan.

The first major block in our plan was getting a good map. Iranians see an espionage plot behind every closed door and one of the ways they try to foil foreign plots is to restrict the issue and distribution of large scale aerial and topographical maps. The only map I had when flying in Iran was a one foot square piece cut from a larger map that showed me how to get to the test flight area and back again. Other pilots were given maps for planning and conducting flights but had to return them when finished.

However, Iranian pilots were careless with their flight bags and we decided to liberate any map we came across that would cover the area from Isfahan to the Persian Gulf. We were all ex-military pilots so we knew the proper frequencies to use when making contact with American ships and aircraft in the Gulf. Within a few days we had two aeronautical maps that covered the desired route. It took us a few more days to get a topographical map from one of the soldiers. Our plan called for us to steal two Hueys, pick their families up on the highway south of Isfahan and escape to either Saudi Arabia or to an American ship in the Persian Gulf. We figured we could get by with it as long as we did it in broad daylight because there was little security during the daytime and departures were not controlled that tightly. Fortunately our escape plan never had to be used.

Terrorism in the City

It was Saturday so I didn't get up too early. I would've normally been on my way to get Christina but I'd found

Ten Months in Iran

out the day before that they were leaving Iran because the demonstrations were getting too violent and too close to where they lived. We had our tearful goodbyes last night during supper at the Kourosh and again when I took her home. Her mother also kissed me and cried when we said good bye. I was sad to see her leave because I had come to enjoy the time I spent with her.

I walked down the alley to the main street and got some fresh-baked bread from the bakery. The bread I liked most was called *lavash* and it was flat, thin, floppy and circular. The bakery didn't supply you with anything to wrap the bread in, so I would just fold it up, stick it under my arm and run home. I liked peanut butter and honey on the hot buttered *lavash* for breakfast. My dog Lucky always sat on the floor beside me and begged for peanut butter. Every morning I would put a big gob of it on my finger and when he opened his mouth I would stick it to the roof of his mouth. He would sit and make the most unusual motions with his head and tongue trying to get it dislodged. Then, he would beg for more and we would do it all over again. Unlike American dogs, Iranian dogs could eat all the scraps that remained from a chicken dinner, devouring bones and all without choking or getting sick. Maybe they just adapted to conditions or the dogs that had a tendency to choke died and didn't pass that gene along. In any case, Lucky would eat anything and he never once got sick.

After breakfast, I cleaned my room, wrote two letters and read some of Mark Twain's book *Letters from Earth*. About noon I decided to walk downtown to eat lunch at my favorite Korean restaurant. This Korean restaurant was one of the best places in Isfahan to get American and Chinese food, and most of the Americans that I knew ate there in the evenings and on weekends. The restaurant

Ten Months in Iran

was also frequented by the British, Canadians and a few Iranians who had developed a taste for good American or Chinese food. There were two big fish tanks in the dining area and one in the front window. They were three feet high, two feet thick and eight feet long. The tanks actually divided the dining room into two separate dining areas and all were parallel to the front of the building.

I sat in the back section for a long leisurely lunch. When I left the restaurant there were about eight or ten people still eating. I stopped outside momentarily while I thought about what I wanted to do for the rest of the afternoon. I decided to walk farther downtown to do some shopping. I was about fifty feet from the restaurant when I was almost knocked down by the blast from an explosion. I turned around and looked back up the street toward the restaurant. What I saw was a sidewalk and street scattered with broken tables, chairs, bodies and flopping fish. The front of the building that had held the Korean restaurant was completely gone. Everyone in the area started running towards the restaurant to offer help so I just walked away. I heard that no one died in the attack, and I think it was due to the large amount of water in the fish tanks; the water absorbed much of the blast.

I spent the evening at Soraya's house talking to her and Sohila about the political situation and the violent demonstrations. I told them how close I had been to the explosion in the Korean restaurant, and I thought Sohila was going to faint. I was never as blunt about the causes of the violent acts as Soraya, but I did always support and agree with her when she was trying to get Sohila to understand what was going on. I think, in Sohila's eyes, this was like two of her best friends were fighting each other and she was just incapable of pointing a finger at one of them and saying 'you are wrong'. She followed me

Ten Months in Iran

out to my car to say goodbye and give me a good-night kiss. I held her in my arms, told her that I loved her and that I wanted her to think about going to the states with me.

The next morning as I was leaving the training facility for the airfield I ran into Colonel Amir in the parking lot.
"Good morning, colonel." I said.
"Good morning, Mister Simpson." he said. "How are you today?"
"I'm fine colonel, and you?"
"I'm Ok." he said. "Would you like to come over to my office and have some tea and conversation?"
"I would be glad to, colonel."
On the way to his office he talked about the hot weather we were having and that he thought it would break soon. He acted apprehensive each time we passed other officers along the way. He was clearly nervous about something. Once inside his office he seemed to relax.
"What do you think about what's going on?" he said.
"I don't know what you mean, sir."
"Come on, Jack." he said. "We're in my office now and we're friends; it's Amir and you know what I mean."
"Ok, Amir," I said. "I think the Shah has an overextended army. I think he has too many enemies and too many people, including my government, who are giving him bad advice. I think the Shah should pick up a very big stick, crack down on the demonstrators, lock up their leaders and find a way to gag the mullahs."
"Well," he said, "I did ask."
The colonel was quiet for a few moments as he drank his tea; then he took a deep breath and started to talk to me.
"You are right and I'm amazed that you have such a grasp on the situation. Where are you getting your information?"

Ten Months in Iran

"Time magazine," I said, "Dad airmails it to me as soon as it hits the street."

"Time magazine," he said, "I'm going to have to start reading it."

"I'll give you my copies and you can catch up on what's been said."

"Thank you, Jack." he said. "I look forward to reading them. However, I wanted to talk to you about something else. Have you kept in contact with anyone in Fort Benning?"

"No, that was too long ago. I don't know anyone there now. Why do you ask?"

"I'm sending my wife and children to the states as soon as I can make the arrangements. My wife liked Fort Benning when we were stationed there and wants to go back. I'm trying to make contact with some family who can help her find a house and watch out for her until this is over."

"If I were you, I would write a letter to the commanding officer of Fort Benning and tell him the whole story. I'm sure the officer's wives organization would be happy to assist your wife and make sure that she's taken care of."

"I need to do this in secret." he said.

"We can do that." I said. "You write the letter and I'll put it into one of my letters home and have dad mail it from Ohio. No one will ever know."

"Thank you, Jack." he said. "I appreciate your help."

"Have the letter ready and I'll pick it up tomorrow."

The next day at work, we were notified that an attack had been attempted on a Bell Helicopter bus that was transporting American workers from one job site to another. The terrorist, riding in an open vehicle, stuck a bomb on the side of the bus as it went past. The workers on the bus, mostly ex-military Vietnam veterans, were familiar with this type of attack and evacuated the bus as quickly as possible. The bus stood in the middle of the

Ten Months in Iran

street for over an hour until a bomb squad from the base could come and remove the device. For one reason or another, the bomb failed to explode.

That afternoon I went over to Colonel Amir's office to pick up the letter he wanted me to mail to Fort Benning. He told me that he had already made arrangements for his wife and children to visit some friends in Turkey for a few weeks and that they would be leaving in about a week. Her brother was driving them to Turkey for what he thought was going to be a short vacation with friends.

"Her brother is what you Americans call 'an asshole'. But, right now, he's a useful asshole; if he knew what we had planned, he would make a lot of trouble for us."

"He's going to know sooner or later." I said.

"Yes, he is. I just hope it's latter, after I'm gone."

"Are you going to ask for political asylum in the states?"

"If the Ayatollah returns and gains power, I'll have to." he said. "Everyone knows that I'm against an Islamic government so, if he returns, I won't be too popular."

I took his letter and inserted it into an over sized letter with instructions to Dad to airmail it as soon as possible, that a man and his family's lives may depend on it.

On my way home that evening I saw a young Iranian girl on the corner of the street leading to the base passing out sheets of paper to the Americans as they left the base. As I drove past she gave me one. It was a notice to all foreigners in Iran from the people of Iran.

Ten Months in Iran

A notice to all foreigners in Iran
Do you all know that why Iranians are getting up and fighting?
Do you know anything about their ideology?
Do you know your role in this country?
And finally do you know why Iranians hate you all so much?
If you don't have anything to say, read this communiqué carefully, because this is our answers to you and all foreigners in this country.

1)   Iranians are getting up against oppression, despotism, colonialism in all means: military, political, economical and cultural.

2)   Iranians are fighting to establish Islamic republic system and they don't mind to devote even their life for their ideology.

3)   In our point of view, Shah is the U.S. puppet and he is the one who carries on all the U.S. orders. So we regard all imperialist and social imperialist countries – especially the U.S. as our enemies.

4)   You are the ones who are carrying on all the imperialist countries orders in our country, and you have direct role in stealing our nation's wealth. The people of Iran hate you a lot and they do their best to get rid of you soon.

5)   Therefore if you think you are a human being quit your job as soon as possible and leave our country other wise you will be blamed for the consequences.

The Iranian People

Ten Months in Iran
Shiite Imposed Demonstration

I did most of my shopping in Isfahan on a little street that was lined with small stalls that looked a lot like the public rent-a-storage areas so popular here today. The shops had no windows or doors, just a pull down garage type door at the front. On a day when all the shops were closed, the street looked like a residential area where everyone had a first floor garage with an apartment on the second floor. During the late summer and fall of 1978 the Shiite mullahs of Isfahan called for all city shops to close on what would have been their busiest money making days. After complying several times the Sunni shop owners were becoming irritated about the money they were losing and decided to stay open. It wasn't long before a mob of Shiite thugs showed up, a few dragged the shop owners out into the street and nearly beat them to death while the others looted their shops and then set fire to them.

I saw the area the next day and about five shops were looted and burned. On a few occasions the Shiite call was only to close early on a particular day that had some political or religious significance. On those days the shop owners who were not in compliance with the order were simply beaten and forced to close.

The U. S. papers cited the shutdown by small business owners as proof of solidarity in the national movement against the Shah's heavy-handed regime. Saying that the Ayatollah enjoyed solidarity in his movement against the Shah is like saying that Hitler had solidarity in his movement to murder the Jews. A citizen's fear of being beaten to death by thugs did not produce solidarity in 1940 Germany and it did not produce it in 1978 Iran. The Ayatollah hoodwinked the people of Iran and when that didn't work, he used fear.

Ten Months in Iran
The Curfew

Every evening at eight o'clock the clear-streets curfew went into effect; then at ten o'clock the power to the city was cut off. Each evening my neighbor and I would stand on the roof and make bets on how soon the first shot would be fired after the blackout. Each night the conflict intensified and the time interval became shorter and shorter until finally the shooting started during the clear-streets curfew. We would stand on the roof and talk, drink coffee and wonder where it would all end. The fighting began on the edges of the city and all we could see were the tracers flying off into the night sky. Occasionally, we would hear an explosion. As the days and weeks passed, the fighting worked its way into the city and to our street. My banker neighbor became too frightened to go onto the roof, and after the second day he sent his family to the country for safety. I think the merchant also went to live somewhere else because I didn't see him after things got bad on our street. I continued to go to the roof every night to see what was going on in the city. I was usually there alone because Tim was too afraid to spend much time on the roof.

It was easy to tell the difference between the soldiers shooting and the young boys shooting: the soldiers had automatic weapons and the boys had only single shot shotguns. That's probably why I never heard of a soldier being killed, although there may have been. The serious fighting usually lasted for about three hours and ended around midnight. The fires that were fueled by old tires and anything else that would burn were out by midnight and the streets were dark. On some overcast nights, you couldn't see anything after the fires went out.

Ten Months in Iran

At about one o'clock in the morning, after the fighting had stopped, a military truck would come down our street and pick up the dead bodies. It took me some time to make out what was making that strange thumping noise as the trucks went slowly down our street. Finally, I realized that the noise was the sound of dead bodies hitting the truck bed. Later, my suspicion was confirmed when an officer walked up to one of the trucks with a flashlight and counted the bodies they had collected on our street. I knew enough Farsi to know that they had collected four boys and one girl. Sohila would always tell me the next day what the radio reported as the official count, and it never seemed valid to me. The reports were always two to five for the city. But I never heard of a single mullah being killed, only idealistic young boys and girls who could be worked into a religious frenzy by the mullahs and then sent out to die.

The American media also did its part to send Iran back into the dark ages. Every article I read lauded the brave Islamic mullahs for their stand against the repressive Shah of Iran. I saw *Time* pictures of mullahs leading peaceful marches in Isfahan and Tehran. Peaceful, you bet they were peaceful. The mullahs didn't want to be on the street if any shots were going to be fired. The media weren't interested in what would happen to the Iranian people or what the Shah had done to improve their lot in life. They wanted only to jump on the popular band wagon and sell, sell, sell add time and subscriptions. *Time* did present a more balanced view of what the problem was and what the Shan was trying to do for his country, but it could have done more. I think *Time* either missed the point altogether or was afraid to report the true nature of the involvement of Iran's radical mullahs.

Ten Months in Iran

No one in the United States or the rest of the civilized world ever had the backbone to stand up and say that the source of the trouble in Iran was the calculated misrepresentation of the Qur'an by radical Muslim mullahs whose objective was to seize power at any cost. They gave no thought to the welfare of the people.

Human Rights and Freedom of the Press

Sohila was translating an article in the morning paper to me about the Shah granting freedom of the press - it was going into effect at noon that day. I knew, because I had read about it in the American morning paper. However, I knew he was granting freedom of the press not because he wanted to but to appease Jimmy Carter, our naïve president. I couldn't wait to see what the Isfahan paper would say that afternoon. We got a paper as soon as it came out and Sohila read it to me. I was not surprised. The paper had such slanderous, outrageous and inflammatory articles that Sohila became embarrassed reading it to me. If something like this had been published in the United States, our government would have arrested the publisher and shut the paper down. The Iranians had freedom of the press for one day. We talked about why the Shah had to rescind the freedom of the press order, and I gave her my lecture about what happens to a society when people are confined and then experience sudden freedom.

I told her that I had learned over the years that you can't drop people into a free society from a controlled existence and expect them to act responsibly and survive. The survival of freedom requires self-control and restraint on the part of the citizens who enjoy that freedom. The survival of freedom depends on citizens who have the character and respect for the law to stop at stop signs even

Ten Months in Iran

though there is no traffic and no one watching. She laughed at that statement.

I told her that I was not necessarily talking about people in Iran but people in general, especially those who have lived in either a communist country or a South American police state.

"People who have lived under total control and who stop at stop signs only because they fear being shot if they don't are likely to run right through the sign when suddenly free of any coercive control. This same attitude extends to almost every aspect of their daily activities. They become almost like children whose domineering parents have suddenly abandoned them."

"I have taken care of children like that." she said. "As soon as their parents leave they turn into monsters. I had no idea it was a natural human trait."

"If you examine the history of any country that has experienced overnight freedom, or the illusion of new freedom, you will find this phenomenon. Freedom requires the self-control and judgment that only time, training and experience within a free society can develop. So, when a country like China decides to make the transition to a free state, the freedoms offered will have to be metered out slowly over an extended period of time or chaos will result and the society will revert back to total communist control or collapse into anarchy. If the Shah would summarily grant total freedom, chaos would be the result."

"So, how are people supposed to become free?" she said.

"Like I said, all of those liberties that make up freedom must be metered out slowly over an extended period of time. Think of it as giving a sick society a medicine that will cure its oppression. You wouldn't give a patient a whole bottle of medicine at one time would you? No, you give medicine to a patient one spoon full at a time until

Ten Months in Iran

the sickness is gone. Freedom is the medicine for oppression; but you can't drink it all on the first day."

"It makes sense the way you have explained it, but I have lived in France where people are free and I didn't go crazy." she said.

"Well, honey, that is something totally different. First of all, you are an intelligent and well bred woman who has enjoyed more freedom in Iran than most people because of your family. Second, it's human nature to act like the people around you. There's an entire section of study on that phenomenon called mob psychology. Basically it says that if you're in a group of people who are behaving themselves, you will behave yourself. If you're in a group of people who are not behaving themselves, you will most likely misbehave also."

"So, I was good because the French were good?"

"Basically, yes. However, through training from your parents you have developed a natural tendency to behave yourself."

"Is mob psychology the reason people are going crazy?"

"People are going crazy in the street because someone knows how to manipulate them using mob psychology."

"How can anyone manipulate a mob?" she said.

"Sohila, there is another extensive section of psychology, probably the most studied of all, and that is psychological warfare. I have studied PSYOPS[17], as the military affectionately refers to it, for years and the more I observe the activities taking place here the more I'm convinced that the mullahs are experts at psychological warfare and subversion tactics. I have often wondered if at least some of them weren't graduates of the Psychological Warfare School at Fort Bragg, North Carolina. If they haven't attended the school, they certainly have read the books because they have implemented psychological programs

---

[17] Psychological Operations

Ten Months in Iran

and executed subversive tactics with great skill and they are producing textbook results."

"Jack!" she said. "Are you trying to tell me that the mullahs are behind all of the trouble we're having?"

"Not all of them. I received my latest copy of *Time* (September 18, 1978) with a picture of the Shah on the cover. While reading the cover story *"The Shah's Divided Land"* my suspicions were confirmed. Some dissidents who found themselves ineffective in recruiting followers due to their inability to communicate with people on a mass scale came up with a plan to exploit the advantages enjoyed by the mullahs. They pretended to be religious and to have a desire to study the Qur'an under the Ayatollah in Qum. And evidently this ruse got them in the door because, according to *Time,* they '*went to Lebanon for training by George Habash's radical Popular Front for the Liberation of Palestine. Returning to Iran, they posed as clergymen, took code names, formed cells and provoked incidents of terrorism.*'

That same article quoted the Shah commenting on priests in South America acting like Communists. He said that '*we can't believe that a priest can become a Communist; but, it is possible that a Communist might get an order to become a priest.*' I think what he really wanted to say, but realized he couldn't, was that we can't believe that a mullah can become a Communist; however, it is possible that a Communist might get an order to become a mullah."

"Who are these men who are pretending to be mullahs; where did they come from?" she said.

"They are Iranians who want to overthrow the Shah's government and they could be communists or just Iranians who want a different government."

"How could overthrowing the Shah's government be an advantage for the communists?"

Ten Months in Iran

"I don't know. Maybe they think they have enough people in high government offices that they can take over during the chaos of a crumbling government."

"Why would the other mullahs let them do that?"

"Well, a majority of the mullahs want the Shah's government to end and I don't think they care how it happens because they believe they can take control."

"What about the Ayatollah Khomeini? What do you think he thinks about all of this?"

"I suspect the Ayatollah knows exactly what's going on and who is responsible."

"How could so many people be caught up in this, thousands of people are demonstrating."

"Sohila, a good psychological operator can take a person who thinks he's happy and making money and turn him into a revolutionary by making his little problems look intolerable and by making his big problems appear absolutely unsolvable, then convince him that all of his problems are the fault of the present government."

"How can you convince people that they have such problems that overthrowing the government is the only solution?"

"With a lot of money and a good platform to deliver your message, a professional psychological subversion operator can convince anyone to jump out of the frying pan into the fire. And the mullahs have all the money they could possibly need and what better platform could you ask for than a Friday mosque?"

"The inadequacy of my government is partly to blame. I'm constantly irritated by its lack of understanding of other cultures and the naïve idea it has that you can just set people free and then walk away. The journey to freedom is a long tough road and it's littered with the dead bodies of countries that tried to make the trip too fast or tried to take short cuts. Being impatient while developing freedom is a killer and people who don't want

Ten Months in Iran

you to make the trip will play on your impatience and lead you away from freedom to a different destination. The people in my government proved during Vietnam that they didn't understand the values, ideals and culture of the Asian mind. Now they're proving that they also don't understand anything about Islam."

Police Brutality

We also talked about police brutality and I told her about one of my Iranian plane captains who didn't show up for work for three days. On the forth day he came to work with his head shaved, sunburned and black and blue from being beat up. He had been arrested for a minor traffic accident and didn't have the money necessary to keep himself out of jail. He told me that everyone who goes to jail gets his head shaved. If the police think you aren't going to be in jail too long they keep you in a cage outside one of the sub-stations.

When I asked how he got sunburned he explained that he was in the sun for three days waiting to get out, and that for the first two days he didn't have any food because his relatives didn't know where he was. He said that if you are arrested and put into temporary detention, you don't get fed unless your family feeds you. He was beaten the first night because he didn't have the money to pay them to get out. Sohila was horrified by my story and couldn't believe that something like that could actually take place.
"I know the police in Iran are barbaric in their treatment of prisoners," I said. "I've heard about prisoners being beaten for little or no reason other than for the entertainment of the guards. I also know that many younger men and boys are sexually abused in jail by the guards. However, I also believe that this barbaric treatment of prisoners is an Islamic cultural problem

Ten Months in Iran

stemming from the fact that most Islamic countries consider people guilty if they are arrested and deserving of any punishment they get from the police or the courts."

"That's not the way our law is supposed to be. Our law says that you are innocent until you are proven guilty," she said. "People must go to court and have a trial."

"Yes, I know, but Arabic custom is, if you're arrested, you must be guilty. Don't get hyper on me now; I know you're Persian, not Arab, but your Islamic customs come from a common root."

"The Shah is in control of everything. He should stop things like that from taking place." She said.

"Police brutality is not the policy of the Shah and he has no method of injecting civility directly into the veins of the police. To stop police brutality would require overcoming the effect of years of exposure to Islamic custom. The Shah could change the system, but overcoming the affect of Islamic custom would be a great deal more difficult."

"I can't believe that police brutality is only caused by Islamic custom. Police brutality exists in many countries all over the world." she said.

"That's true." I said. "However, there is a big difference. Police brutality here is a systemic problem related to your culture. Police brutality in the United States is a personal problem. There will always be some police brutality because police are people and people have problems - the degree of brutality depends on the type and severity of the police officer's problem or problems. If a police officer has a fight with his wife before he goes to work and then has to arrest someone who is resisting, it is human nature to vent your anger on someone who has unknowingly volunteered himself as a target. The degree of abuse will depend on the degree of severity of the argument with his wife. He may only slam the suspect down a little harder

Ten Months in Iran

than required or he may slam him down and then kick him in the head."

"Why do you know so much about this?"

"My dad was a police officer and I have heard many his stories about, and explanations for, police brutality."

"Was your dad ever brutal with a criminal?"

"I don't think dad was ever brutal with anyone, but I suspect he did on occasion use a little excess force when arresting a wife beater of any other abuser of women. He took a hard line with anyone who abused a woman and I think it was because his sister was once a victim."

"I have always been taught that every problem has a solution, so this problem must also have a solution." she said.

"The Shah is trying to solve the problem by adopting a more Western style of justice and legal system, thereby moving away from the old Islamic type of tribal justice and its severe, excessive and inappropriate punishment of minor crimes. A man should not be thrown into jail and have all of his hair shaved off for a minor traffic accident. Iran is not there yet and it will take time to re-educate the police. In the mean time, trying to blame the Shah for police brutality would be like trying to blame our president for the brutality of a Mississippi sheriff beating up on a prisoner. Neither the president nor the Shah operates on that level of management. I'm sure the Shah knows about police brutality; I'm also sure that he has much bigger and more urgent problems that demand his time."

News of Farah

Jay came by my classroom and motioned for me to come to the door. He looked pale and I thought he may have been crying.

"What's up?" I said.

Ten Months in Iran

He looked at me for a moment without saying anything. I could tell he was trying to compose himself. I had never seen Jay when he was not in full control of his emotions, so I suspected something had happened to Mai.

"Farah's dead!" he said.

He stopped and tried to get control of his emotions.

"What do you mean, she's dead? How?"

"I just talked to Mariam and she told me that Farah committed suicide two weeks ago. She said Farah was so upset about being away from Tom that she didn't want to live."

"I wonder if she committed suicide or if her family murdered her."

"Who knows?" He said. "In either case, she's dead."

"You're not going pass this news along to Tom, are you?"

"I couldn't even if I wanted to. He's never contacted me since he left for the states." he said.

"If you do hear from him, don't say anything about her death; it's something he doesn't need to know." I said. "It would only drive him deeper into despair."

"That's not the worst part of the news."

"What could be worse than that?"

"Mariam was the one who told them about what she was doing." he said.

"Oh, my god!" I said. "Why would she do that?"

"Her parents suspected something from the tone of Farah's letters home. Evidently she sounded too happy and contented. So, her father sent Mariam a threatening letter that if anything happened to his daughter, he would kill her. So, she broke down and admitted that she had a job and was working. They didn't find out about the boyfriend until her uncle got here."

"Why did she confess to you?"

"Because she feels guilty about Farah's death, she thinks it was her fault. I'm afraid now that she may kill herself. I tried to talk to her and tell her that she had no choice but it

Ten Months in Iran

didn't help. I've never seen anyone in so much mental agony; I was afraid to leave her alone."

"My god, isn't Islam a wonderful religion?" I said.

"Well, Jack," he said, "I don't think Islam has a monopoly on intolerance. My parents almost killed my sister when they found out she wanted to marry a black man, they sent her away to a boarding school."

I returned to my class and continued to teach, but my thoughts were on the three beautiful lives that had been tragically destroyed. I couldn't stop think about Tom, Farah and Mariam.

Receipt for Disaster

The overall situation in Iran, and in Isfahan in particular, were deteriorating daily. The demonstrating crowds got bolder and bolder in their efforts to destabilize the government. It was evident that new and more experienced leaders were taking charge of the demonstrations. I attributed this escalation to the fact that during the two preceding years, the Shah's secret police SAVAK had identified and arrested scores of individuals responsible for inciting riots and committing terrorist acts. They identified the people of the press who were distorting the facts to further incite the public and arrested them or restricted what they could print. However, our State Department at that time tried to get the Shah to treat the problem (the people's lack of a political voice) and not only the symptoms (public dissent).

The Shah unfortunately was slow to act on this advice. Now, with President Carter in the picture, the United States had different priorities. Carter's crusade for human rights pressured the Shan to not only turn loose the identified and jailed dissident leaders, but also give them a free press so they could disseminate their insightful lies and half-truths to the public. This one move by President

Ten Months in Iran

Carter did more to de-stabilize Iran and eventually dethrone the Shah than any other action by any other group. If a genie had appeared before the Ayatollah in Paris and offered him three wishes, his first two wishes would have been for the freedom of his jailed dissident leaders and for freedom of the press. Carter proved to be the Ayatollah's magic genie and granted his first two wishes. I think the Ayatollah's third wish would have been that Carter would continue to be an inept President; Carter also granted him that wish.

Ten Months in Iran

Chapter 6
Soraya's Dinner Party

Soraya called me after work on Friday and invited me to a dinner party at her house. She said she had a surprise for Mahmoud and me. When I arrived at seven o'clock Mahmoud was already there sitting on the floor with Soraya. Sohila and I sat down on the floor together and shared a pillow.

"Where is the surprise?" I said.

"You will see it in a few minutes," Soraya said.

"Do you know what the surprise is, Mahmoud?"

"I don't have a clue. She won't tell me either."

Soraya and Sohila excused themselves and left the room to check on the food. About five minutes later they came back and said that supper was ready.

"What do you mean, it's ready?" I said.

We were sitting in the room where we had always eaten. This was the room where I had had my first complete Iranian supper served while sitting on a Persian rug.

"Follow me gentlemen." Soraya said.

She opened the door to the room that had been her oldest son's bedroom and invited us in.

"Surprise!" She said, as she stepped back to show us her new dining room, complete with table and chairs.

"Soraya," I said. "This is a beautiful setup. When did you get it?"

189

Ten Months in Iran

"It was delivered yesterday."

"Why did you do it?" I said.

"Well, I know it would make you two feel very important if I said I did it for you. But, I did it for me. I have found out that I enjoy what I'm eating more and feel better after eating at a table. The whole process is easier on my back."

"What do you think about it, Sohila?" I said.

"I love it. It's easier to set up, easier to serve and easier to clean up after you're finished."

The four of us had a long and enjoyable meal followed by a bottle of good wine. Reza came home just before we left the table and greeted us before retiring to his room. His mother offered to fix him something to eat but he said he was not hungry.

Mahmoud and I retired to the family room while the women cleared the table. A few minutes later Sohila came in, turned on some classical music, and sat down beside me. In another minute or so Soraya came in, turned out the lights and sat down with Mahmoud. The only light in the room was from the moon and stars illuminating the garden. It felt so good to lay there in the dark and hold Sohila in my arms. Every time I close my eyes and kissed her I was almost overcome by the sensation that we were being molded together like two pieces of soft clay. That sensation, along with the scent of her perfumed hair and the heat from her body, was narcotic.

"As much as I hate to break this up," Mahmoud said. "We only have thirty minutes to get home before the curfew."

Soraya got up and turned on the lights. I stood up and offered Sohila my hand to help her to her feet.

"Ok, Mahmoud." I said. "This was your idea and you are the only one still on the floor."

"It really wasn't my intention, and I didn't expect, that everyone would jump up and be ready to run out the door."

Ten Months in Iran

I knew all along why he hadn't jumped up with the rest of us by the way he was clutching the pillow around his groin. I also had an erection earlier in the evening but the little guy gave it up when he figured out that nothing was going to happen.

Reza walked into the room and announced that we might as well sit back down because he had just heard on the radio that the army had moved up the curfew because of all the demonstrators who were already on the streets.

"It looks like you'll be spending the night." Reza said.

"How can we spend the night here?" I said.

"Simple," Soraya said. "We just keep doing what we have been doing for the past hour. But, I think it would be a good idea if we had a little snack first."

Soraya and Sohila went into the kitchen to fix something to eat and Mahmoud and I sat back down.

"Good," Reza said. "Now we can talk. I found some old Iranian coins that I want to give to you. I found them in the bazaar last week but this is the first time I've seen you. I'll go get them."

"You two really get along together." Mahmoud said.

"Yes, we do. We have a similar interest. We both like to collect coins."

"You get old coins at the bazaar?"

"Yes, and you can find coins from just about any country you want. I have found and purchased old American coins here for one tenth of what they would cost in the states."

"What countries do you collect coins from?"

"I originally just took coins home as souvenirs from countries I was stationed in while in the service. After awhile my collection got so big that I decided to get serious about it. But I still only collect from countries I have lived in."

"How many countries have you lived in?"

"Seventeen." I said.

"You have lived in seventeen countries?"

191

Ten Months in Iran

"Yes," I said, "and also the Arctic and Antarctic."

"I think you had a more interesting career in the service than I did."

Reza returned with five old Iranian coins he had found in the bazaar and gave them to me.

"Oh, these are beautiful." I said.

"They're old special edition coins and they're hard to find anymore."

"Are you sure that you don't want to keep them?"

"No, you keep them. I have a set already."

Sohila returned from the kitchen and set up a place for us to eat on the rug.

Just then we heard a distant explosion and the faint sound of gunfire. Sohila looked at me and for the first time I could see fear in her eyes.

"It has never been close enough for us to hear before." she said.

Soraya came quickly into the room. She, too, had a look of fear in her eyes.

"Did you hear that?"

"Yes, we did." Sohila said.

"Why are they coming this far out into the neighborhoods? There's nothing out here for them to protest against." Soraya said.

I suspected they were coming out into this neighborhood because this was an enclave of educated and well-to-do people, liberal intellectuals who were considered the enemy of the revolution. I did not tell them that.

"I think they're just trying to get more people involved." I said.

Mahmoud gave me a look that told me he knew what I was doing and then agreed with me. Soraya and Sohila got the food from the kitchen and we sat down to eat. Everyone was very quiet for a long time as we sat and listened to the noise and gunfire in the distance.

Ten Months in Iran

"That was excellent, Soraya." I said. "If I keep eating like this I'll have to go out and buy new clothes."

"Thank you, Jack."

The room got quiet again as the ladies cleared the food away.

"Well, if they're going to put on a show, why don't we go up on the roof and watch it while we drink our coffee?" Mahmoud said.

"Good idea." I said. "I'd like to see which direction they're moving."

"You two go on up and well get the coffee." Soraya said.

"Are you coming up with us, Reza?" I said.

"No, I have things to do in my room."

Once on the roof and out of range of the ladies, Mahmoud and I had a confidential talk.

"Do you think we should try to get them to go to their father's house?" Mahmoud said. "He lives in the country and they would be safer there."

"I don't think Soraya would leave her house; she's so proud of it," I said.

"Yes, I know. That's a problem. She'll want to stay here and protect her property even though she can't really protect anything."

"If we tried to stay here with her and there was any trouble it could cause an international incident. Americans clashing with Iranian freedom demonstrators, we could spend the rest of our lives in jail or we could be lucky and they would just kill us." I said.

"You're right, that's not an option."

The ladies came up with the coffee and we stood on the roof and watched the glow of fires that were not more than three streets away. There were explosions in the distance but nothing close. The demonstrators seem to have been moving parallel to our street and were now getting farther and farther away. After thirty minutes we

Ten Months in Iran

could not hear them anymore. But we could still see the glow of the fires they had caused.

"Let's go back downstairs." Soraya said. "I'm getting tired."

We assumed our original places on pillows on the rug. The lights were already off due to the city-wide blackout enforced by the army. I didn't sleep much that night. Sohila slept soundly in my arms all night. During the night I noticed that Mahmoud and Soraya went to her bedroom for about an hour and he came back alone.

Soraya was up at dawn and in an extremely good mood as she prepared breakfast for everyone.

"Why don't we just go for a drive in the country today?" Soraya said.

"Sounds good to me," I said.

"I'm in," said Mahmoud.

"Sohila," I said, "would you like to go for a ride in the country?"

"I'll do what ever you want to do."

"I know where there are some ancient ruins and a Zoroastrian fire temple west of the city; and I know Jack is interested in the Zoroastrians." Soraya said.

Soraya and Sohila went to the kitchen to get some food ready for the trip and Reza took Soraya's car to get some gas. We decided to take two cars due to the security situation caused by the demonstrators. We didn't want to get caught on the road after dark if the car broke down. Soraya and Mahmoud went in Soraya's car and Reza, Sohila and I went in my jeep. I let Reza drive, I sat in the front and Sohila sat in the back. We figured this was the safest configuration for the trip since I had an open jeep. Mahmoud was driving Soraya's car but he could easily pass for Iranian as long as he didn't open his mouth. I, with my white skin, blond hair and blue eyes, didn't have a chance of passing for anything except a foreigner. I

194

Ten Months in Iran

thought I might try to pass myself off as a German but with my luck I would run into an Iranian who could speak German and he would know right away that I was faking it.

I never knew where we were at because we didn't have a map and, of course, all the signs were in Farsi. We went through two pitiful little mud hut towns on the way - the site and smell were beyond belief. Each time I was astounded by the thought that the Ayatollah had actually convinced these people that they should fight against the Shah's efforts to modernize Iran. They are fighting for the Ayatollah who would keep them where they are for the next thousand years.

As we traveled west along the road I was happy that Soraya had packed some food, otherwise we would have starved to death because there were no *Wendy's, McDonald's* or *Burger King's*.

The Zoroastrian fire temple was off the right side of the road on top of a rocky hill. It was a tough climb up the hill and we were all sweating when we got to the top. The most impressive thing about the temple was the fact that it was made from camel dung, straw and dirt and most of it had survived for two thousand years. Then I remembered a stone block bridge in Rome that the Romans made over a thousand years ago, without cement, and it is still in use today. And we can't even make a steel bridge in Ohio that will last a hundred years.

We located some shade and decided to eat there before going back. Mahmoud and Reza made the trek to the cars for the food while the ladies and I sat in the shade. There was a nice breeze blowing and it, and the shade, made the 90^0 air temperature feel quite pleasant. We had a quiet meal beside the temple and then started back.

195

Ten Months in Iran

It was late in the afternoon when we arrived at the city limits where we ran into a line of about fifteen cars that were stopped at a road block set up by the army. The soldiers were turning some of the cars away from the city. I was happy to see it was an army road block and not a civilian road block because Mahmoud and I had Iranian army identification cards. The situation got tense when the men in the car directly ahead of us got into an argument with the soldiers about being denied entrance into the city. The two men got out of their car and confronted the two soldiers manning the check point.

After arguing for a few seconds one of the men pushed the soldier he was arguing with and the soldier leveled his rifle at the man and shouted a command to him. The man put his arms over his head but continued to argue and walked toward the soldier. I saw the man who was arguing with the second soldier reach under his shirt and pull a gun from his belt. I told Sohila to get down on the seat and cover her head. The first soldier who had his gun leveled at his antagonist saw the gun being drawn and immediately killed both men. Both soldiers were now in an extreme state of agitation and having seen soldiers in combat and agitated, I knew this was an intensely dangerous situation. I told Reza and Sohila to be quiet and not move. Mahmoud and Soraya were in the car behind us and I was sure he was telling Soraya the same thing. We sat there for several minutes listening to the soldiers arguing with each other over what to do. Finally they pulled the bodies to the side of the road and moved the dead man's car off the road. They argued with each other some more and then just waved all the remaining cars through the roadblock.

"That was too close to even think about." I said.

"What happened?" Sohila said.

At that point Reza and Sohila did something they had never done before; they talked excitedly for several

Ten Months in Iran

minutes in Farsi. Reza was flushed and shaking from the incident and Sohila turned pale at the thought of what had happened. Mahmoud, in the car behind us saw everything but Soraya sitting in the passenger seat saw nothing.

I couldn't tell if Reza and Sohila were just having an excited conversation or of if they were arguing during the remainder of the trip home. If I had to put any money on the conversation, I would bet that Reza was behind the soldiers and that Sohila was telling him that no one should ever be killed. I had Reza pull over and stop so I could go back and talk to Soraya and Mahmoud.

"Are you two ok?"

"Yes," Mahmoud said, "wasn't that something to write home about?"

"We were lucky it wasn't any worse than it was."

"Why did they shoot those two men?" Soraya said.

"One of the men pulled a gun on them." I said.

"Do you two feel like having supper at the Kourosh? Or, are you too worn out?"

"The Kourosh sounds like a good idea; I could use a drink." Soraya said

Everyone was quiet for a long time after we sat down in the club restaurant and placed our orders. Finally, Reza broke the silence.

"I've never seen anyone killed before except on television. I didn't know guns were so loud."

"I can't believe this is happening here." Sohila said. "Has everyone gone mad? We're supposed to be civilized people. Civilized people don't kill each other."

"Jack and I have been trying to tell you how bad it is and what is going to happen if the Shah is deposed; but you won't believe us." Soraya said.

"I'm sorry, but I just can't believe that the mullahs are behind this. Mullahs are not murderers." Sohila said.

Ten Months in Iran

Everyone was quiet again for a long time and then Mahmoud decided he would try to explain to Sohila what was happening.

"Sohila," Mahmoud said. "Neither Soraya nor Jack is saying that the mullahs are directly involved in causing the death of people. They are not claiming that the mullahs are murderers. They are saying, and I agree with them, that the mullahs are guilty of agitating and inciting people to riot. If you don't believe what I say is really happening, look closely at the news the next time they are covering a Friday demonstration that starts after prayer at a mosque. If the mullahs are leading or attending the demonstration, it will be peaceful; if there are no mullahs in sight, the demonstration is going to be violent."

"How do the mullahs know if the demonstration is going to be violent?" Sohila said.

"I'm so glad that you asked that question." he said. "They know because they know how much they have incited their audience. They know because they know just how far to go to cause a demonstration and how far they have to go to incite a riot."

"The demonstrators come from many different mosques and have been listening to many different mullahs." she said.

"That only proves what I say is true; and that is, they are all following orders from one central point. They are all following the same master plan drawn up and directed by the Ayatollah Khomeini."

The table fell silent again as the food arrived. We remained quiet for the remainder of the meal.

Mahmoud and I had just enough time left to get the ladies home and get home ourselves before the eight o'clock curfew.

Ten Months in Iran
Friends Leaving

During November and December of 1978 there was a mass exodus from Iran. Men were either sending their families home or going home with them. Bob and his family left Iran and after they got back to Alabama, Bob got a job doing something in Red Lodge, Montana. I received several letters from Christina from their new Montana home. She wrote that her father had to sign legal papers that said he would continue to support the Iranian man injured in the accident after he returned to the United States or they would not let them leave the country. Her father had hired a lawyer to look into the problem.

The Pilipino Nurses

Amelda's good fortune with her job at the hospital didn't last too long because the government, in an attempt to appease some dissidents, started expelling foreign workers who, they said, were parasites and taking up jobs that Iranians could fill. The hospital let her go and she didn't get her bonus. I never got to talk to her before she left, so I had no idea where she went.

A few weeks later Mai left Iran because she also lost her job at the hospital. Jay quit Bell Helicopter and took her to the United States. I received a letter from Mai a few weeks later telling me that they had gotten married before continuing on to visit her relatives in the Philippines.

My Neighbors

When the banker found out that a lot of Americans were leaving Iran he asked me if his children could have Lucky. He said they were in the country and would not be coming back until all of the trouble had stopped. I gladly

Ten Months in Iran

gave my dog to him and was happy to see Lucky get a good home. I can only hope that the banker's wife and family escaped from Iran before the Ayatollah took control of the country, otherwise I fear she may have been executed or jailed; I was almost sure that I was not the only one to whom she had expressed her feelings about the Ayatollah.

I know the merchant didn't leave town because I continued to see his automobile in his courtyard and I could tell that it had been moved. But we never again had our roof-top talks after the demonstrations made it to our neighborhood. I suspect he was doing whatever necessary to survive.

Asking for Sohila's Hand

I called Soraya one evening and asked if she could stop by my house because I wanted to talk with her about something. When she arrived I told her that I was in love with her sister and wanted to know if it was alright with her if I asked Sohila to marry me. She was extremely happy about my proposal and immediately said it was alright with her. I asked her if she thought Sohila loved me enough to marry me. She assured me she did and that they had already talked about the possibility of my asking for her hand. I told her that I felt like I should ask her father but since I hadn't ever met him I decided to ask her. She told me that it was perfectly acceptable because she was in charge of her sister. I asked her if her father would approve of the marriage and she told me she thought he would be happy about it because it would get her out of Iran and into a country where she could continue her education in whatever field she wanted. I knew she wanted to be a teacher of languages.

Ten Months in Iran
Islam's Hypnotic Power

Sohila had a deep compassion for everything that was alive - dogs, cats, birds and people. She had a conviction for the sanctity of life that I had previously seen only in Buddhists. Every death, for whatever reason, was a needless tragedy to her. We had several talks where I tried to get her to see why the differences in opinion between the mullahs and the moderate Iranians were being blown up into problems of apocalyptic proportions by the mullahs. They were doing it to justify a violent overthrow of the Shah's government. She couldn't see the duplicity that I saw in the mullahs who were agitating the Shiite mobs with one hand and supposedly trying to calm the situation with the other. She was certain that they were honest and sincere in their leadership and that their only objective was to create a free and democratic Iranian state. I would really like to talk with her again now after the Ayatollah Khomeini's thugs have been in power for twenty years.

This was the most logic defying social movement that I have ever witnessed in my entire life. Young Iranian women, who liked the fact that they didn't have to wear a black sheet over their head if they didn't want to, were fighting for the Ayatollah who would force them wear the chador. Under the Shah they could attend parties and go dancing, things they loved to do. Now they were fighting for the Ayatollah who would outlaw parties and dancing.

The young Iranian men who loved to chase non-Muslim women (and there were plenty of foreign women available in Iran) and frequently caught them, were now fighting for the Ayatollah who would stop them from catching any woman. All of Iran's young people loved to listen to Western music, watch TV, dance, drink and go to the movies. But they were fighting for the Ayatollah who would outlaw all of these activities. Yet, they chose to fight, and many of them died, for an Islamic State that would stop them from doing everything they loved to do. As Spock of *Star Trek* would say - 'festinating'.

Help from the United States

Jimmy Carter couldn't have planned a better strategy for deposing the Shah. He set up a scenario for deposing the Shah that any psychological warfare operator would be proud to claim credit for. First, he pressured the Shah into releasing political prisoners. Second, he pressured the Shah to allow for free assembly. Now, the dissidents would be able to assemble and agitate the population in preparation for overthrowing of the Shah. What a beautiful set up! The result was an escalation in the opposition to the Shah and the escalation was viewed by his enemies as a weakness.

Student Demonstrators

Iran's extensive and well-organized Shiite clergy apparatus took its orders from the Ayatollah Khomeini in Paris, and those orders were to keep the opposition alive and growing. Some university students, working under the direction of Shiite mullahs began coordinated and well financed street demonstrations. The American media put great stock in the fact that university students were demonstrating against the Shah, as though the students were privy to some insider information that the general population didn't have. The fact is, it's easier for mullahs to grab and control the minds of idealistic and impressionable young university students who haven't yet been exposed to the realities of life than a man who has a wife and children to support. How did the mullahs sucker

Ten Months in Iran

the students in? They told them they would create a modern, up-to-date Islamic State where men and women would have equal civil rights in a modern Iran and that they would create a modern educational system, one that everyone could enjoy.

The mullahs also wanted to provide the people with a free press, something that, according to the mullahs, was not allowed under the Shah. The mullahs promised a democratic Islamic state where the people could elect their leaders. What they didn't tell them was that after the people had elected their leaders, the Ayatollah would then tell the elected leaders what to do. If he didn't like them or they refused to do what he said he could dismiss them from office.

By this time the Shah was unable to stop, or even slow down, the demonstrators who were instigating violence to inflame the situation. Then, after a violent confrontation, they would provide the media with proof of atrocities that fit their propaganda objectives.

Back in April, Moscow joined President Carter in pressing the Shah up against the wall when Russia instigated a coup in Afghanistan. This opened the door for subversives to across the Iranian border and infiltrate Shiite mosques. It also caused the Shah to divert some of his troops to that area away from the cities where he needed them. Before the Shah was out of the country there were Soviet backed Afghanis in Iran setting up terrorist camps.

Iran's Never Ending Plight

Iran's problems didn't start with President Carter. Iran's religious problems started 2600 years ago and its political problems started 100 years ago when the West first took

203

Ten Months in Iran

an interest in Iran (called Persia at the time) and its resources. Russia moved into Iran from the north and the British moved in from the south from India. Persia had no central government or army to keep foreigners out because it was populated by groups of mutually hostile tribes divided along geographic and ethnic lines. The strongest tribe was the Qajars, but they were never able to pull the other tribes together to form any strong central force. The lack of any unity in Persia made it easy for Russia and the British to move in and dominate the country. The Qajars, in an effort to survive and become stronger, cooperated with the foreigners.

The religious leaders felt threatened by Western culture and ideas that came with increasing foreign domination. The Russian economy set up in the north and the British economy set up in the south had devastating effects on the traditional Persian economy and the bazaaris lost control of there markets and customers. The intellectuals liked the idea of a liberal government; the educated and secular-minded wanted to borrow the best aspects of the West in an effort to combat despotism, religious traditionalism and foreign control.

The people were not happy with the leadership the Qajar monarchy and the situation finally came to a head in 1906 with protests and confrontations brought religious, secular and liberal groups together to force the creation of a parliament and a constitution. The parliament soon became so bogged down in tribal feuding and competition between the political groups that a legislative stalemate resulted.

In 1911, the Russians pressured the Qajar to dissolve the parliament, which effectively divided the country into tribes again causing anarchy to exist through World War I. The Russians left the country when their own revolution started.

Ten Months in Iran

In 1921, Reza Khan, with British backing and three thousand followers, took Teheran. He also increased his popularity by putting down tribal fighting and general lawlessness. He was initially minister of war and then became prime minister.

In 1925, after he got rid of the last surviving tribal king, he made himself Shah of Persia. He took the name Pahlavi from pre-Islamic Persia. It is thought that he took the name Pahlavi to indicate his intention of having a non-Islamic secular outlook on governing Persia, an outlook that did not please the Muslims. He ruled Persia and then Iran after the name was changed.

In 1941, he was forced out by the British who favored his twenty-two-year-old son, Muhammad Reza Shah.

In 1945, after World War II, the United States became interested in Iran because of its strategic position in relationship with the Soviet Union. The U. S. became Iran's best ally, providing it with arms and training to develop a strong military force. However, the United States failed to see the true nature of Iranian society and made some serious political and social errors in dealing with Iran.

In 1949, the National Front party tried to reestablish a democratic government with a parliament and a constitution similar to 1906. Serious problems came out of their proposal to nationalize the oil industry because the British had a lot of money invested in it.

In 1951, the idea of nationalization was so popular that Iran soon became the first Middle Eastern country to nationalize its oil industry.

In 1953, the West boycotted Iranian oil forcing the Shah to denationalize the oil industry.

To overcome his enemies, the Shah (with the help of the CIA) created SAVAK, a secret police force. SAVAK became the most feared agency in Iran, it was feared by internal as well as external enemies.

Ten Months in Iran

In 1972, the Shah deployed helicopters and pilots to help Prime Minister Zulfikar Ali Bhutto of Pakistan put down a revolt of the Baluch tribe. Since there are about one million Baluch in Southeast Iran, this action created more internal enemies for the Shah.

In 1973, Iran once again took control of its oil fields.

We, along with the English, are paying for the sins and short sightedness of our fathers concerning the Middle East. After World War II the English drew arbitrary borders in the area that is now Iran, Afghanistan and Pakistan. The new borders paid no attention to loose tribal borders that had been observed for centuries. The Baluch tribe had a very large area called Baluchistan, but the English divided the Baluch tribal area up without consideration of the location of the tribe. Now the members of the Baluch tribe are divided between Iran, Afghanistan and Pakistan.

Other Middle East tribes like the Kurds were also divided up arbitrarily then their tribal land was assigned to Iraq, Turkey and Iran. The division of these tribes and the loss of their autonomy, whether it was real of imagined, has been the source of constant Middle East trouble. Most of the desert tribes in the Middle East hated each other because they were competing for the same resources. It has always amazed me that we haven't figured out yet that you can't put three or four of these tribes in a bag, shake it up, call it a country and walk away expecting it to survive.

Even though the United States was a staunch supporter of the Shah, it frequently undermined his authority and credibility by giving him poor advice. Many times the advice given was calculated to make the U. S. president look good at home more than to solve a problem in Iran. The Kennedy and Carter administrations both fall into this category. It's questionable how well the State

Ten Months in Iran

Department understands Iranian society, considering the advice they have given over the years.

Reza Shah and Muhammad Reza Shah spent their lives trying to drag Iran out of an eighteenth century agricultural economy and establishing it as a twentieth century industrial economy. The Shah's modernization program and the poor advice form the United States created new and powerful enemies. His newest and most powerful enemy was the Ayatollah Khomeini. Khomeini's protest movement became so popular in Iran that the government arrested him in 1965 and exiled him to Paris.

To Khomeini, the Shah was the source of Western contamination of Islam through his alliance with Western governments. He saw the Shah and the upper-class Iranians transforming Iran into a secular society. Khomeini's objective was to overthrow the Shah, purify the society and create a righteous government with himself as the pious leader, a leader who could ensure that the people would do God's will.

Ten Months in Iran

Chapter 7
Come with me Sohila

I asked Sohila if she would marry me and return to the States with me. She said that she would love to marry me and go to the United States, but she was worried about what would happen to her father if she were to leave Iran. I told her that we could take him with us, but she informed me that her father would never agree to leave his home. I could see what was in store for Iran and Soraya could see it too, but we couldn't get Sohila to see what we saw. Over the next few weeks I talked to her and her sister talked to her but we couldn't get her to leave her father even though Soraya promised to take care of him. Near the end, Soraya became almost frantic. She told Sohila that if she went to the United States first that it would open the door for her later and that she really wanted out of Iran. Sohila believed every word the Ayatollah Khomeini reportedly said even though Soraya and I both told her that the local mullahs were making up most of the things she was reading in the paper that were attributed to the Ayatollah just to gain support for the revolution.

Belief Trumps Education

As educated and intelligent as she was Sohila believed the Ayatollah Khomeini's promise that he would not enforce

Ten Months in Iran

the old chador edict that required all women to wear the chador in public. She also believed his message from Paris that he would set up a truly Democratic Islamic State where the people would elect the leaders who would then represent them in the government. My American-educated banker next door also believed the same story. What fools, I thought, as I listened to each of them tell me how wonderful it would be when they finally had an Islamic government. The Ayatollah Khomeini and his mullah followers had the people of Iran so mesmerized with promises of a free press, improved economic conditions and a representative government that they could not see what was always lurking in the fog of religion - the Ayatollah's desire to have absolute unlimited control over them. There is one, and only one, reason for religion and that is control of the population and the more fanatical the religion the more unlimited the control.

We have police to enforce civil laws. However, if you want to do something illegal you may not get caught if no one is watching. So, tribal leaders have always done what my Mother did when I was a young boy and she couldn't be looking over my shoulder all the time. She would say that God was always looking at me. I couldn't get away with anything because God was always watching me and He would send me to hell if I did anything wrong. I didn't want to go to hell for breaking a streetlight or stealing some ice cream from the corner store so I behaved myself. She also told me that if I did what God wanted me to do that I would be rewarded after I died. Mom knew what she was doing. Islamic mullahs have taken this idea to such an extreme level that it is beyond the comprehension of Western and European societies. They have convinced the fools that listen to them that God's ultimate reward is given to those who commit suicide by blowing themselves up while killing innocent people.

Religion may very well be a necessity in the maintenance of a well-run society. We need though, to watch those wielding the power of religion to ensure they do not abuse their position and totally subjugate the people they are supposed to be leading. Preachers, mullahs, priests and rabbis are only men and, if not held in check, will make up rules to serve their own agenda.

One Last Try

One Saturday afternoon as I was reading in the living room, the courtyard door opened and Sohila walked in alone. I met her at the front door and asked her where Soraya was. She told me that Soraya had dropped her off and was going to see her boyfriend. I was so surprised that I didn't know what to do. I asked her in and sat her down on a chair across from the sofa where I had been sitting and got her a cup of coffee. I expressed my surprise about her being there alone and she told me that Soraya wanted us to have some time alone so we could talk. I was very uncomfortable. I knew that Soraya wanted us to get married and maybe she was giving me one last shot at convincing Sohila to go with me. So, I jumped right into it by asking her if she had changed her mind about my proposal. She said she was thinking about it but hadn't yet changed her mind. I decided to alter my tactics and stay away from any negative arguments, since they hadn't worked anyway. I said that I wasn't a rich man but that I had a good education and had earned a lot of money in the past and would continue to earn a lot of money in the future. I told her that she could go to any college or university that she wanted because I could find work anywhere.

Ten Months in Iran

I also told her that once she and I were situated in the States we could send for her father and sister. She explained again that her father would never leave Iran because he wanted to be buried next to his wife. I explained to her that even if he died in the States he could still be buried in Iran. I asked her if marrying someone who is not a Muslim was bothering her and she assured me that it didn't make any difference to her what religion I was and that she wanted to marry me, not my religion. She came over to the sofa, sat down beside me and asked if I would stay in Iran with her. I told her that I would love to stay in Iran with her if the Shah remained in power. I told her, however, everything points to the Shah being deposed and the Ayatollah taking over the country. I told her that the situation was going to be intolerable after the Ayatollah took charge and that with my belief, or lack of belief, I would not be safe in Iran under a religious government. I could see she was disappointed with my answer.

I moved to put my arm around her and she snuggled up to me. I held her for several minutes and neither of us said anything. She shifted around and looked up at me. I looked at her expecting her to say something. She said nothing. She was so lovely. Her face was a contrast of color with her very light skin, black hair, dark eyes and deep red lips. I pulled her to me and kissed her gently, holding it for a long time. I could feel her body responding to my touch; she put her arms around me and pulled me closer. As we kissed the passion began to build. I reached inside her blouse, pushed her bra strap off her shoulder and took her large firm breast in my hand. Her breathing became heavy as I fondled her breast and continued to kiss her. It wasn't very long until I began to feel light headed and my fingers started to tingle. I was breathing so hard that I was hyperventilating. I had to

211

back off and rest. When I relaxed and sat back she asked me if any thing was wrong. I told her that nothing was wrong, that I was just getting too excited. She pulled closer to me again and threw her leg over my lap. I put my hand behind her knee, pulled her leg farther up onto my lap and ran my hand up her skirt. At that point she pulled up her skirt and sat down on my lap. I unbuttoned her blouse and noticed that her bra had the catch in the front. Now both of her breasts, glistening slightly with perspiration, were free for me to enjoy. She had very small, very dark and very hard nipples. Her breasts were absolutely symmetrical and her nipples, like two dark eyes, were looking directly at me. As I placed my mouth over one, I could feel it getting larger and, once again, I had an erotic response to the taste of her perspiration. After several more minutes of heavy petting and kissing, I moved my hand up between her legs and under her panties where I discovered that she had removed all of her pubic hair. She must have used some chemical method of removing the hair because her skin was soft and smooth. There was no trace of stubble. As my fingers continued to explore the most private parts of her body I gently massaged her clitoris before moving to the entrance of her vagina where I made another discovery - she was a virgin. That discovery released such a flood of thoughts and images into my head that I had to stop. She asked me again if anything was wrong. This time I had to think about my answer.

If she were doing this to get me to stay, it wasn't going to work. I can't speak Farsi and I'm very poor at learning a foreign language, so I would be helpless if I tried to get a job. She will not leave her father and come with me so there isn't much hope for this relationship to work out. A twenty-five year old virgin; I couldn't believe it. I thought for sure she would have been caught by someone before now. Her sister and her father can't be with her twenty-four hours a day. A raging battle was going on in my body between my hormones and my conscience. I loved Sohila and didn't want to cause her any trouble when she did find an Iranian man that she wanted to marry. I didn't give a shit whether the woman I married was a virgin or not; but, the Iranian who will some day marry Sohila will want her to be a virgin, and she will be.

I thought the best way to handle this was to tell her the truth. So I told her that I didn't think we should go any further than we had because we were not married and by the way things were working out, it didn't look like we ever would be. I told her that I wanted her to be a virgin for the man she would someday marry. Then she asked me if I still wanted to hold her and kiss her. I said I did want to hold her and kiss her for as long as I could, and if she would come home with me I would hold her and kiss her for the rest of my life.

Time to go Home

I realized that the situation in Iran was getting close to the critical point and decided that it was time for me to leave while I could still get out. I talked to Tim and he said that he was already talking to friends in Saudi Arabia to get a job there teaching English to the Saudi army. He expected a job offer within a few days. I went to the American Army captain who was my immediate supervisor and told him that I had decided to go home. He told me that he hated to lose me but that he understood. He admitted if he could go home, he would.

Next I went to the headquarters building and told the area director that I wanted to go home. He said he would initiate the paperwork for me and that he would need a

Ten Months in Iran

final Employee Performance Review from the captain. When I saw the captain later that day he had already made out my review and wanted to go over it with me in his office at about noon the next day. I performed my last three test flights that day, and was sad because I knew that I would probably never fly a Cobra again. This was a final goodbye to something I loved.

I found Mahmoud, told him that I was going home and asked him what he was going to do.

"I've been corresponding with my old boss in Texas about getting another job supporting operations on the oil rigs in the Gulf. I think he's going to hire me again. He understood why I came over here and we parted on good terms."

"I am so glad to hear that, Mahmoud. That's one more testimonial why one should never burn bridges you leave behind."

"How about you, what're you going to do when you get back home?"

"Well, I really don't have to jump through my ass to do anything," I said. "I get a retirement check from the Army every month. I've been giving it to mom and dad to help them out while I've been over here."

"I've been sending my mom and dad money too, but, I don't have any retirement, unfortunately." he said.

"I'll probably get a job in Columbus as a technical writer. There's always work in that field and it pays well."

"What does a technical writer do? And, where did you learn how to do it?"

"That's something I learned to do in the U.S. Navy as an electronics instructor. Navy instructors had to write their own lesson plans and student support material that was to be passed out in the classroom."

"What did you teach?"

Ten Months in Iran

"I was an AT[18] before they broke the rate up into all the branches[19] that exist today. I taught radar, communications, navigation and electronic counter measure equipment at the navy's advanced electronics 'B' school in Millington, Tennessee."

I gave Mahmoud my address in Ohio, and he gave me his address in Texas, so we could keep in touch after we both got back to the states.

The next day I had a message from personnel to pick up my exit package, a list of things I had to do to get out of Iran. At noon I went to the captain's office and went over my performance review with him. I had never become friends with the captain because he was always busy and our paths didn't cross except in the office where I picked up my test flight assignments. However, he had obviously been watching me. In his review he said "one of the most professional test pilots I have known, sums up Mr. Simpson's performance. His devotion to his profession is tireless and enthusiastic and I want him back. Mr. Simpson should be rehired on immediate request."

One of the areas on the form asks for an area of improvement and it specifically says that an entry of none is not acceptable. The captain entered, "Mr. Simpson has a very low tolerance for bullshit."

I laughed out loud when I read that and the captain said, "Well it's true, and that was the only thing I could think to put there."

I signed the review and the captain sent it to personnel for approval.

That afternoon I started to work on the long list of items I was required to complete before Bell Helicopter and the

---

[18] Aviation electronics Technician
[19] The Navy separated the ATs into the fields of communications, navigation, radar etc.

Ten Months in Iran

Iranian government would let me leave the country. I had to get my landlord's signature on a note saying that the rent was up to date and I had not damaged his property. I needed a signature and note from the telephone company and the car leasing company saying that I did not owe them any money. That took care of the government. The to-do list from Bell was a full page and would take me two days to complete. I had to check out with the tool crib, flight gear issue, school, mailroom, flight line maintenance, flight line locker room and finally with personnel to turn in my airbase ID card, get my final pay, a ticket home and my passport. My flight to London was a week away so I would have time to spend with Sohila and to say goodbye to everyone.

I had picked up a trunk the previous day and packed away all my things to be sent home; the last thing I did before leaving the base was to deliver the trunk to the Bell Helicopter shipping office.

I felt a little sad when I drove through the gate for the last time. I had, after all, enjoyed my job and the people I got to know. It was kind of like watching a movie that you really did like, but turned out to have a bad ending.

Two Parting Gifts

My practice of keeping my extra money on hand, in Marks and gold, paid off because in December, the demonstrators raided the banks frequented by Americans. They broke all the clay tablets containing the bank deposit records, then burned the buildings. I only lost the few hundred Rials that I kept in the bank so I could maintain an account there. Tim, who always thought I was crazy for keeping my money in cash, lost several thousand Rials.

Ten Months in Iran

Before I left the country I could tell that Soraya was getting anxious about her financial situation because she became very conservative about buying anything and she started talking about the cost of gas for her car. She and I had talked about keeping money in a safe place for emergencies and I know that she also purchased German marks to keep her stash money from being eaten up by inflation. I felt sorry for Soraya because she was a woman who was caught up in events that she couldn't control and couldn't escape. On the day that I left Iran I gave Sohila one of my $300 dollar gold coins and told her to keep it in reserve just in case things got bad. I also gave her a poem that I had written for her. I put it in an envelope and told her not to read it until I was gone and she was alone. Now, I just had to accept the fact that our relationship didn't work out the way I had planned.

217

Ten Months in Iran

Sohila's Poem

Lead me, Sohila, to that room of jade
Where pleasures that Sultans die for is made
    And I pledge my love to you from this day
Until beneath this Couch of Earth I'm laid.

My love's like the pomegranate – bittersweet;
I come to her fountain to drink and eat;
    Oh! Sweet invitations – bitter delays;
She plays games with me and I fear defeat.

Her eyes reflect a fiery russet glow,
Like the mountains capped with a winter's snow
    And lighted by the late evening's red sun;
Passion fires my lover's eyes – Oh, I know.

You're a lover with a thousand faces,
Now cold, like the wind through mountain passes;
    Then hot, blowing across the desert's waste;
Me? I search … for the distant oasis.

Come, love, throw your garments down in my tent;
And after an evening of love we've spent,
    We'll eat and drink and talk of life and things;
Then retire anew to love's enjoyment.

Ten Months in Iran

Chapter 8
Back Home

On my first evening back home I turned on the evening news and listened to Walter Cronkite to find out what was happening in Iran. What I heard made me gasp in disbelief. The radical Muslim mullahs were spreading lies about the Iran situation and NBC, CBS and ABC were scooping up those lies and spoon-feeding them to a gullible American TV audience, an audience that believed that "if it's on TV it must be the truth". What were the lies? I'll list them for you:

First Lie: Walter Cronkite told the whole United States that the outlying villages in Iran were revolting against the Shah because they had no running water or wells and that they had to have water trucked into the villages.

The Truth: the Iranian Government, under the Shah's direction, spent years developing water systems in the countryside. The government dug wells, installed pumps and built water distribution pipelines in hundreds of villages across Iran.

Second Lie: Walter Cronkite reported on the evening news that the desert people (nomads) invaded the city of

219

Ten Months in Iran

Isfahan causing riots that killed innocent bystanders. He said the nomads were demonstrating against the Shah.

The Truth: The desert people came into Isfahan almost every weekend to trade and buy supplies (they did not invade the city). On this particular weekend the mullahs had the Shiites worked up against the Shah and they were demonstrating against the government. As the demonstrators moved through the city they came into the park where the desert people were camped. The desert people were staunch supporters of the Shah and the two groups got into a horrific argument that led to intense fighting. The city fighters did not fair well since the desert people were all armed with knives and swords.

The Third Lie: Walter Cronkite reported that the Shah was making no effort to make land available to the common people and that only a few rich people in Iran owned the majority of available land. I suppose this was to insinuate that the rich people were all friends and relatives of the Shah.

The Truth: Most of the land in Iran was (is) owned by a few rich people (the mullahs) who dupe wealthy land owners into leaving their property to the mullahs so that they will be afforded a special place in heaven. The mullahs then sharecrop the land and collect the money. As I said earlier, the Shah was in the process of buying land from the mullahs and distributing it to people who would eventually own the land they worked. The mullahs were outraged by this because the Shah was setting the price that was paid for the land at exactly what the mullahs claimed it was worth on their tax statements (even though the mullahs operate tax free).

Ten Months in Iran

That was the last time I ever listened to Walter Cronkite report the news. As far as I was concerned, he had lost all credibility as a reporter.

A Friend Executed

While listening to the evening news I learned that Colonel Amir Abdul Ehya, the Iranian colonel with whom I had built a friendship, was executed by the Ayatollah as an enemy of the Islamic State. He either waited too long or something happened to prevent him from leaving the country and joining his wife in Turkey. I know she made it to Turkey with the children. Now I can only hope that she and the children made it to Georgia and were given political asylum. During our last conversation I could tell he was in fear, not so much for his own life, although he knew his life was in danger, but for the lives of his wife and children.

Trying to Locate Old Friends

In 1990 an Iranian friend of mine told me that he was going to go back to Isfahan to visit his relatives. I gave him Soraya's address and asked him to see if he could locate Sohila. I was anxious to know what had happened to her and her family. When my friend came back he said Soraya's house was run down and empty and that the neighbors told him she had lost both her sons in the Iran-Iraq war, and one day she just never came back to the house. He asked about Sohila and they said they hadn't seen her since the war and didn't have any idea what happened to her.

Ten Months in Iran
Jay and Mai

Mai and I corresponded for almost two years after we left Iran. I frequently asked her about Amelda, but Mai had no idea where she was. Mai's last letter informed me that she had divorced Jay because he wouldn't get a regular job and that she had left him in the Philippines. She was working in Korea as a nurse and being treated well.

Letters from Christina

There was a graduation picture enclosed in the last letter I ever received from Christina. She was all dressed up, had makeup on and had cut her long red hair. She looked beautiful. She told me that she had graduated and was leaving Montana to live with her aunt in Hawaii. She also told me that her father's lawyer, Bell Helicopter and the State Department got him out of paying any more money to the Iranian for the traffic accident. I wondered what life had been like for her in Montana after being in Isfahan. She should have been able to write some good reports about 'what I did last summer'.

Letters from Mahmoud

I got only one letter from Mahmoud, saying he was going to go to work for an American company as an air operations officer servicing the oil and gas rigs in the North Atlantic and that he would be working out of Norway.

Priscilla

I never heard from Priscilla after she returned to the states. I think she was like a bird that had been kept in a

Ten Months in Iran

small cage and was now free; I think she took flight and never looked back.

Maggie

Some of the wives somehow got the word about Maggie and complained to the company. I think the Iranians may have also complained because I heard that she was terminated and sent back to the states before her contract was completed. I have always had a deeply felt sorrow for Maggie; she was a troubled lady who, I think, was looking for something that she will never find.

My Performance Review

About a month after I got home I got a copy of my Bell Helicopter Employee Performance Review in the mail and found out that someone in the personnel office cleaned it up by changing the captains entry about my having a 'low tolerance for bullshit' to 'expresses complaints too readily'. The new review lacked my signature.

My Trunk from Iran

The trunk that I packed in Isfahan and delivered to the Bell Helicopter warehouse for shipping never made it to the United States. When the government fell, the warehouse was sacked and more than a thousand trunks were stolen. Although I lost all my clothing, a Persian rug and around forty books, the two things that bothered me the most were the loss of a picture album that contained ten years of school pictures of my five daughters, and the loss of my special collector's edition of the *Rubaiyat of Omar Khayyam* that Sohila used when she read to me.

Ten Months in Iran

Epilogue

The Islamic governments of Afghanistan and Iran have come closer to creating the negative utopia described in George Orwell's *1984* than the communists. The mullahs have also emulated the pigs in George Orwell's *Animal Farm* by fermenting a revolution and then becoming more repressive and ruthless than the regime they replaced. Their success can be only attributed to the fact that the mullahs have brainwashed and mesmerized their Islamic followers since birth. Islamic radicals have lost their ability to think for themselves and must consult a mullah every day to see what they should be thinking about and what stand they should take on any given idea, subject or problem.

They are like mindless zombies who are susceptible to any suggestion and will follow any order given by a mullah. They beg and even die for the privilege of being placed under a clerical dictatorship. The Islamic Iranians who were not radical were duped into believing the Ayatollah Khomeini's promise of a democratic government where the people would elect the leaders who would then make the laws. What they didn't know was the Ayatollah's concept of a democratic government was a system where the people elected their leaders and then he would tell the elected leaders what laws they could and could not pass according to his interpretation of the Qur'an. In fact, the Ayatollah Khomeini was a clerical dictator sitting on top of a pretend democracy. The government of Iran could have been changed without the bloody revolution, but a peaceful evolution would not have placed the Ayatollah in charge and that was his only objective.

President Carter

Most Americans voted for Jimmy Carter because he was a good Christian boy, but he was a catastrophe as a president. I also know that people didn't like Nixon because they thought he was a crook. However, if I had to pick between two men to be the president of the United States and one was like Carter and one was like Nixon; I would pick the one like Nixon. Nixon was a good foreign policy president; Carter was a terrible foreign policy president. He was too innocent to work on the world political stage.

He closed several international doors through his excessively simple-minded and quixotic approach to human rights. He evidently was unaware that you can't jerk a sovereign country around like a dog on a chain.

His impatience and naiveté set the people of Iran back a thousand years. The loss of Iran as an ally and as a stabilizing force in the Middle East was a major contributing factor in the Iran-Iraq war and the U.S. having to go to war with Iraq in Desert Storm.

Carter cut off or cut back any foreign aid to countries that didn't live up to his standard of human rights, so instead of making things better for the poor people in some country in Africa or South America, he exacerbated the problem. But, I suppose it gave him some kind of psychological rush to know that he was standing on the moral high ground. We need to conduct our foreign policy based on mutual self-interest and then try to talk the wayward countries into being more humane to their people.

Religion and Politics

One thing I have learned by living and working in Iran is the necessity of keeping your religion and your politics in two separate pockets. Even living under the Shah, who was trying to filter religion out of politics, it was impossible to draw a line between the two. I became painfully aware of why our founding fathers declared that church and state must be kept separate. How can you campaign against someone's politics if he claims, and some believe, he is God's messenger. If we ever elect a zealot who claims to know exactly what God wants us to do, we will lose our freedom without a shot ever being fired. Once in power, how do you challenge a religious politician (I like to call them religiticians) who some believe is executing God's will. Some of my friends have asked me if I pray and I tell them that I do pray. I pray every day that God will save us from religion.

A final thought

After being exposed to the method the mullahs' use in presenting the Qur'an to Middle-Eastern Muslims I can not help but see a parallel between that process and Plato's allegories of *Line* and *The Cave* (books six and seven of Plato's Republic).

Plato's allegory of *Line* basically divides one's perception of information into two categories: valid and invalid.

Ten Months in Iran

Valid information comes from knowledge and reason; invalid information comes from opinion and belief. Middle-Eastern Islamic mullahs spend their lives preventing their followers from crossing the *Line* from the belief/opinion side to the knowledge/reason side. They accomplish this by telling and convincing their followers that they are incapable of understanding the meaning of the Qur'an and must therefore depend on a mullah's interpretation to be fully informed about the meaning of any particular passage. This is where the process parallels Plato's *The Cave*.

Plato's allegory of *The Cave* presents a situation where people are confined from birth to a dark cave and forced to develop their concept of the world from shadows cast on the cave wall by some unspecified superior being. The shadows that are cast onto the wall are not from real things, but from cardboard cutouts. So, the people in the dark cave develop their concept of the world from the shadows of the two-dimensional cutouts made to represent three-dimensional items. The people in the cave are satisfied with their lives because the cave is the only life they have ever known and they're incapable of imaging a different existence.

To the people confined to the cave, the shadows are real objects; they talk about the shadows and agree on names for the shadows. The shadows are their reality. In the cave the shadows are created by a fire that the people can't see; so, they know nothing about where the shadows are coming from. To the people in the cave the shadows are real and they exist independently on the wall.

One day, a man escapes from the labyrinth into the daylight world outside. He's initially blinded by the sunlight, but he becomes acclimated after a while and is able to see what is around him. At first he's terrified and

Ten Months in Iran

amazed by the three-dimensional objects, color and surface shapes and textures. He recognizes items by their outline and he now knows what a tree really looks like. After overcoming his excitement and initial curiosity, he decides to return to the cave and tell the others about his discovery.

Back in the cave he tries to convince the others that there is a world outside the cave and tries to describe the things he has seen - the sunlight, the color and the beauty of a better world. His fellow cave dwellers don't believe him and get tired of his insistence that there is something better, so they kill him. They're happy with the shadows on the wall and are satisfied with their life in the cave, a life they understand.

It is not possible to set any Islamic fundamentalist free because their minds have been bound, gagged and enslaved by the chains of Islam, chains forged from the Qur'an by despot mullahs.

The End